Jane Shutt is a leading practitioner of shamanic healing and a popular leader of workshops about shamanism. She lectures for the Pagan Federation and is a regular contributor to *Sacred Hoop* and *Spirit Talk* magazines. Her work takes her all over the world, from Europe to Hong Kong and the United States.

the SPIRITS are ALWAYS with ME

True Stories and Guidance
from a Modern Shaman

Jane Shutt

RIDER

LONDON · SYDNEY · AUCKLAND · JOHANNESBURG

1 3 5 7 9 10 8 6 4 2

First published in 2003 by Rider,
an imprint of Ebury Press, Random House,
20 Vauxhall Bridge Road, London SW1V 2SA

Random House Australia (Pty) Limited
20 Alfred Street, Milsons Point, Sydney,
New South Wales 2061, Australia

Random House New Zealand Limited
18 Poland Road, Glenfield,
Auckland 10, New Zealand

Random House South Africa (Pty) Limited
Endulini, 5A Jubilee Road,
Parktown 2193, South Africa

The Random House Group Limited Reg. No. 954009

Papers used by Rider are natural, recyclable products made
from wood grown in sustainable forests.

Printed and bound by Mackay's of Chatham plc, Kent

Typeset by seagulls

A CIP catalogue record for this book
is available from the British Library

ISBN 1-8441-3049-5

CONTENTS

••••••••••••••••••••••••••••••

1. What is Shamanism?   1

2. The Shamanic Universe   13

3. Shamanic Healing   31

4. Soul Retrieval   47

5. The Land of the Dead   71

6. Elemental Spirits   93

7. Haunting isn't Always Done by Ghosts!   110

8. Working with Spirits of the Land   129

9. Rabbits, Jackdaws and Blue Hares   147

10. Where Do I Go from Here?   158

    Epilogue   163

Appendix: Core Shamanic Practitioners' Circle Code of Ethics 165

Useful Addresses   166

Further Reading   168

Index   169

To Christine

. . . .

CHAPTER ONE

WHAT IS SHAMANISM?

    I walked slowly along the path. On either side heather moorland stretched far away to a blue and cloudless sky. The sun shone. I had no idea where the path went, nor what I might encounter along the way.

    Far in the distance I could see a bird flying towards me, as yet too far away to recognise the species. All I could see was that it was big. I continued to walk forward and soon I could see that it was an owl. It landed in front of me and looked at me.

    I said, 'Can you show me where to find my Teacher?'

    The owl flew off along the path, back the way it had just come. Once it turned, but, when it saw I was following it, it flew on without checking again. It flew quickly but somehow I kept up with it.

    Then, suddenly, we were at a cliff. I stopped just on the edge. Below me the chalk dropped to a stony beach. The tide was either in or very nearly so.

    I became aware that a man in a black robe stood beside me.

    I said, 'Are you my Teacher?'

    He nodded, smiled and the skin around his eyes crinkled. I felt as if this were someone I could trust.

    I asked, 'What are you going to teach me?'

    He pointed down to the grass growing beneath our feet.

    'That is earth,' he said.

    He pointed to the sea.

    'That is water.'

    He raised his hand to the blue sky.

    'That is air.'

    Then to the sun.

    'And that is fire.'

It's many years since I did that first shamanic Journey where I met my first Teacher and my first power animal helper. I still have little idea where the path goes, or what I might encounter along the way. But I know that I walk that path with my spirits and I know that, wherever my path takes me, the driving force that moves me along it is shamanism.

This book is about shamanism. It's not a 'How to do Shamanic Journeying' book, nor is it esoteric ramblings designed to mystify. Ever since I started teaching shamanic workshops people have asked me to recommend books on the subject to them. There are a few books I suggest. But there isn't a book that clearly explains what shamanism is and what people can expect if they visit a shamanic healer or attend a shamanic workshop. So I would like to try to fill that gap.

'Shamanism' has become a very popular word recently. This can mean that some people know the word without knowing quite what it means. They often know that it is a spiritual path that reveres nature, or that it has something to do with Native Americans, but finding out more is not always easy.

Shamanic practitioners do indeed revere nature and hold it sacred. But so do many other people who would not consider themselves 'shamans' or 'shamanic practitioners'. And, while there are many Native American peoples, such as the Pomo or the Salish, who are shamanic, there are also many, like the Navajo or the Hopi, whose beliefs and practices are not shamanism.

Shamanism is found all over the world, in every continent. Even though organised religions have replaced shamanism for many of us, either by persecution or by assimilation, there are still cultures that are primarily shamanic.

It has been stated, often, that shamanism is the belief system behind all religions – the first spiritual practice. It is probably the oldest spiritual path in the world, believed by many anthropologists to date from the Palaeolithic. Piers Vitebsky describes shamanism as 'a cross-cultural form of religious sensibility and practice' rather than a religion in itself. Shamanic cultures all over the world have their own religious beliefs, practices and deities. There are, in the UK, shamanic Christians, Buddhists, Muslims and Jews. There is no central doctrine, no world church, no holy book and no system of priesthood. Somehow, it seems much easier to say what shamanism is not, rather than what it is.

And yet, there are definite practices and beliefs that shamanism includes. First is animism. This is the belief that all things have soul. Understanding what 'soul' or 'spirit' means is a huge philosophical, psychological and theological argument. All I can say to you on this subject is that to me the spirits are entities – friends, enemies, acquaintances – that I meet and can speak with. Some people are more at ease talking about 'essences' or 'energies'. This is fine, although sometimes we can replace one word with another without any advance in understanding.

We were teaching an introductory workshop and I had been speaking about the spirits. I am a very pragmatic person and I tend to talk about the spirits as I do about other people. Some are wiser than I, some are not. Some are cleverer (not necessarily the same as wiser), some are not. Some are moral, some are immoral and some are amoral.

One of the students said to me, 'What are spirits?'

This is a very difficult question to answer. Each of us perceives things in our own way.

I asked, 'What words can I use that you will understand?'

He said, 'Are they energy?'

'Isn't everything energy?'

'Are they energy?' he demanded again.

Well, if everything is energy, then spirits are, but I don't really feel that this clears up the entire mystery.

I said, 'If I said that the spirits are energy would you understand all about them?'

'Yes,' he said, so I said:

'Yes, they are energy.'

He was happy and, as far as I can tell, there is now a man in North Yorkshire who understands the spirits and who can define them precisely.

But I can't. To me they are a wonderful mystery and a precious gift, and I treasure their mystery.

This belief that everything has spirit is known as animism. But this is a basis for religious belief, not a religion in itself, any more than monotheism or atheism are religions. Shamanism can be, however, and is for me, a spiritual path followed without any more formal religious beliefs.

Another belief that shamanists share is that our soul or spirit can, at times, leave the body. This happens automatically at death. It can happen at other times, for example if we are sleeping and dreaming, if we are very ill or if we suffer severe trauma. The shaman can send out his or her soul to the spirit realms intentionally. This is the shamanic trance Journey. And this is what defines whether or not a practice is shamanism.

The word 'shaman' comes from the language of the Evenki, a Tungus-speaking people who hunt and herd reindeer in Siberia and northern China. It is pronounced 'shaa-mann' with the emphasis on the second syllable. It was among the Evenki that Russian anthropologists first documented shamanism in the nineteenth century and, by a hundred years ago, the word was being used to describe people from other cultures who did the same work. In any shamanic culture the shaman Journeys to the spirit realms, to communicate with the spirits and to return with power, healing or knowledge for the community. In the spirit worlds he or she will meet with spirits whose task is to help the shaman to heal or to advise the community or to bring the rain, or whatever it is that the shaman is seeking.

Of course, many people are aware of or even communicate with spirits without being shamans. Much work with spirits, for example by spiritualists, is done without Journeying. Shamanism is distinct from many types of trance mediumship. The shaman is always in control of his or her Journey – not, of course, in the sense that he or she directs events. The shaman directs what the shaman does. The spirits direct themselves – but in the sense that the Journey is always undertaken with an aim in mind, and the shaman chooses when to go. Spirit possession is not shamanism. Nor is astral travel.

In native shamanic societies the shaman works for the community. There is no such thing as a 'lone shaman'. Evenki shamans operate within Evenki society. Salish shamans, from the northwest coast of North America, operate within Salish society. If we practise shaman-ism here then it must be within our society. It must have a place within our culture, just as it has in any other culture. Shamanism is not a New Age word. It cannot be used to mean anything other than has been described. It has a precise meaning both to the Evenki and to anthropologists and therefore should have to us. I do not believe that we have the right to take a word from another culture and change its meaning simply because we like the word, or we like the reactions of our friends if we call ourselves 'shamans'.

For many years anthropologists, studying shamanic cultures, dismissed shamans as 'charlatans' or 'madmen'. But, gradually, anthropologists realised that if they were ever to understand shamanism they would have to experience it themselves. Michael Harner was one of these anthropologists. He learned to shamanise from the Shuar of Peru, then brought what he had learned north to the USA and formed the Foundation of Shamanic Studies to study shamanism in all its forms worldwide. He coined the phrase 'core shamanism' to describe this worldwide shamanism without cultural or religious overlays.

Core shamanism is, therefore, the common threads of shamanic practice from all over the world. It is the heritage of everyone, wherever they live, whatever their ethnic or cultural background or religious beliefs. On our workshops it is those common threads that we teach. This is not because we believe that shamanism should, or could, be practised in a cultural void, but because we are a part of our culture, just as the Inuit shaman is part of his. It makes no more sense to me that someone born and brought up in the United Kingdom should learn to practise Nepalese shamanism than someone born and brought up in Central Africa should practise Mexican Huichol shamanism. We each belong to our own cultures and to the lands where we live. So 'core' means that central part of shamanic practice that is not dependent upon cultural traditions. But to most core shamanic practitioners it means more than this. It means also that shamanism is 'core' to our practice and to our lives.

We don't live in a shamanic society. That is self-evident. But does shamanism have a place in this society? Well, if it didn't, then the spirits wouldn't co-operate with us, and no amount of our teaching would enable you to meet them. So, what place does it have? In hunter-gatherer societies shamanism is traditionally used to locate

5

game and to appease the spirits of the hunted animals. In agricultural societies the shaman works, for a large part, with the spirits of the weather and of the crops. And here? Now? Well, the shaman has always been a healer and shamanic healing is still a large part of the work of contemporary shamanic practitioners.

But there is more to it than just this. I feel strongly that there is a need now for a spirituality which can return us to a harmony with the land and which can promote balance within ourselves as individuals, but which also acknowledges that we live in an industrial society with all its attendant problems and advantages.

For me, and maybe for you, that need is met by shamanism. After reading this book you may want to try shamanism for yourself. In that case, go on a workshop. You won't be committing yourself to becoming a fully-fledged shaman, but you may well find a path that will change your life.

My life has changed considerably in the years since I first started to study shamanism. I was a schoolteacher, living in Nottingham, when I became interested in seeking a spiritual path. Like many people I had sought for something other than a materialistic view on life at several times in my life. I was lucky in that my parents, both deeply moral and compassionate people, were atheists and did not have any religious world-view to give me. When I therefore decided that there was something more to existence than straightforward Ordinary Reality, I was not limited by previous experience or a pre-existing belief system. (I'd better explain something here. Castenada's terms 'Ordinary Reality' and 'Non-ordinary Reality' are in common usage among shamanic practitioners. This material world in which we live most of our lives, not seeing or communicating with the spirits, is known as 'Ordinary Reality'. When we shift consciousness during the shamanic Journey, to the state where we can interact with the spirits, we call where we are 'Non-ordinary Reality'.)

Being so unlimited, I started, in my teens, by investigating various types of Christianity. Most of my friends were Church of England and I tagged along with them to services and Sunday schools. One close friend was a Roman Catholic, another was a Quaker. Later I met Jehovah's Witnesses, Unitarians and people with other broadly Christian views.

I have been very fortunate that into my life have come a wide range of people with a wide range of beliefs, from those early Christian friends, through the Jews, Buddhists, Hindus, Muslims and Pagans I met in Nottingham to my brother's wife and my sister's husband, both of whose Chinese backgrounds have given me a yet wider perspective on spiritual matters.

But these interests and perspectives, although valuable, did not speak to me as paths that I could follow with a clear conscience. And then I discovered shamanism.

To begin with shamanism was presented to me as an integral part of the Native American Medicine Wheel, something that I now realise reflected simply the tastes of the person teaching me. And it seemed to be a series of interesting techniques that had no really deep spiritual meaning. I came home from the workshops and taught my partner, Christine, to journey. But that was all.

Then, gradually, it became more. My spirit helpers, not limited by the notion that they were supposed to be a North American construct, began to talk to me of ways in which to lead my own life. I did some reading and discovered that, far from being a few techniques that originated on the other side of the Atlantic, shamanism was something that was the heritage of everyone, worldwide.

One Easter holiday I went to the Lake District with Christine for a week. Like me, Christine was a secondary school teacher. While we were there we Journeyed. Christine came back from her Journey white and shaken. These are her words.

A pupil at the comprehensive school where I worked was murdered by his stepfather. A few weeks later I was on a routine journey to Non-ordinary Reality when this happened:

Suddenly I was aware of a grey mist to my right. I looked and, to my astonishment, recognised Andrew – the murdered schoolboy – inside the mist. He moved towards me and spoke. 'What's happening, Miss? What have I done wrong? I'm sorry, Miss.'

I was speechless with a mixture of horror and pity. My spirit helpers bowed their heads; they had no help to offer.

'I'm sorry, Miss. I didn't mean to do whatever it was. You love me, don't you?'

I found myself answering him. 'Oh Andrew, you've done nothing wrong, nothing at all. Don't worry now. Everything will be all right. Everyone loves you.'

He looked at me so piteously. 'But I'm so alone,' he said. 'I'm frightened. What will happen now?'

I was now aware of a bridge of rainbow lights and colours stretching up from where we stood, on a beach, away up into the clouds. It seemed people were up there in the clouds imploring Andrew to join them. I pointed to them.

'Look, Andrew – all those people love you. They are your ancestors. They want you to join them so that they can take care of you.'

He looked up at them and stepped back in alarm. 'How can I get there? I'm so frightened. I'm so cold. Let me stay here with you, Miss. Please.' I was desperate. I had to help Andrew, but I didn't know how to do so.

'Look – how about going over the bridge with one of my spirit helpers?' I suggested encouragingly. 'They'll look after you.'

He shook his head sadly. 'No. After we get to the top of the bridge they'll leave me and I'll be alone again.' My spirit helpers bowed their heads still further. I had no idea what to do.

Then instinctively I stretched out my right arm – it seemed to go on for miles. I touched something, held it and brought it back. It was a rabbit. I gave it to Andrew. His face lit up with joy as he held the rabbit close. 'This is for you,' I told him. 'Your rabbit will look after you and stay with you always.' Andrew smiled at me then turned and walked happily and confidently up the bridge and away. My Journey ended and I returned to Ordinary Reality.

After that experience I was reluctant to Journey again. I had been thoroughly shaken up and frightened by what had happened.

It took Christine nearly a year before she dared to Journey again, in case Andrew reappeared. I took the problem to the man who ran the workshops that I had been attending. He had no help to offer. He did not know how to deal with the spirits of the dead, nor did he have any advice for us.

This marked a turning point for me. I knew, from my spirits and from my reading, as well as from Christine's Journey, that shamanism was a much deeper experience than I was being taught at the workshops. I had a long talk with my spirit helpers and, with their blessing, began the unbelievably hard task of trying to move forward alone.

I don't recommend this. Of course, we need time that is just between ourselves and our spirits, but without the guidance of a community we easily become directionless.

Eventually, after about a year, when I was at a very low ebb in my spiritual search, I came across a leaflet advertising one of Jonathan Horwitz's basic workshops in shamanism.

Jonathan lives his shamanism. I may not agree with every nuance of what he says but his message comes from his spirits rather than his ego. I came home from the workshop and suggested that Christine go to the next one that Jonathan held, six months later. We both found the guidance we needed, from Jonathan himself and from the deeper way in which he encouraged us to relate to our spirits. Shamanism moved, for me, from being clever techniques to being a spiritual path along which I could walk for the rest of my life.

The spirits told us to stop teaching in schools and to move north. Although I am from Sheffield originally and Christine is from Carlisle, we have family on the edges of the North Yorkshire Moors, my parents live in Guisborough, to the north of the moors, and Christine's parents, until their recent deaths, lived on the coast at Scarborough. The spirits led us and found us a house, within our price range, in Rosedale, right in the centre of the moors. And then they started pestering me to teach shamanism. I prevaricated for just over a year, but they were becoming insistent. And so, in the summer of 1997, Christine and I formed the North Yorkshire Shamanic Centre and began to teach shamanism and to give shamanic healings. We now have far less money and somewhat less leisure time than we had before, but the rewards are enormous in other ways.

Be warned, although it is quite possible to satisfy your curiosity and attend one workshop and then no more, I know of no one whose life has not been changed when they started to take this path seriously. Although these changes have turned out for the best in the end, not everyone is looking for change. All spiritual paths challenge us and transform us. Think carefully. Is this what you want?

As I said before, this is not a 'how to' book. I strongly feel that shamanism, even basic Journeying, is something that is best done in experienced company. I said before that I taught Christine to Journey, long before I began to take shamanism seriously. I was lucky. Christine found it hard to do at first, taking weeks to manage a Journey to meet her power animal, but when she did, nothing went wrong.

On the first Journey of one of our students, Katy, the call-back (the drumming sound that signals to the Journeyer that it is time to come home) sounded, but she did not return. She said later, 'I heard the call-back and turned to come back up the tunnel, but I couldn't find my way. There was just sea all around me.'

It took nearly ten minutes of panicking for her to struggle back to Ordinary Reality.

Another student, Carol, was Journeying when the telephone rang, jerking her back to her living room. She was disorientated and frightened. It was not until we investigated later that we found she had left a part of herself in Non-ordinary Reality.

Accidents happen, even on well-run workshops. But, on well-run workshops, there is someone there with the knowledge, experience and connection with their spirits to sort out the problem, to lead Katy home or to re-unite Carol with herself.

Workshops have other advantages. On workshops the vast majority of attendees manage to Journey within the first day. For those learning from a book and trying the techniques for themselves, we have met only one or two who managed it. Time after time I hear students say that they have used a book but have not got anywhere.

On workshops you hear other people's Journeys. This helps to validate your own experiences. Don't underestimate this. We do not live in a society that automatically validates shamanic experience.

And on a workshop you have the chance to ask all those questions that you can't put to the author of a book.

It is perfectly all right to Journey by yourself once you know what you are doing, but I would strongly advise you to be taught in the first place by someone who is experienced and who knows how to teach.

Of course, I don't want to put you off reading books about shamanism! A good book – and I hope that this is one – will give you an introduction to the subject and a feel for whether this is a path that you might want to try. One of the things I've tried to do in this book is to describe a wide range of different people's experiences. Reading around any subject is a good idea. But it's an addition to, not a substitute for, a well-run workshop.

So what actually happens when you go on a workshop? Well, I'll describe some of the things that are likely to happen if you come on one of our workshops. Other teachers, of course, teach in different ways and have different priorities.

First it is likely that you'll have a short talk about shamanism and have a chance to put your questions to the teacher. Of course, if you have the kind of burning question upon the answer to which may hang whether or not you want to continue with the workshop, I suggest you telephone the teacher and get your answers before you part with your money.

Then you are likely to get an introduction to your first Journey, which will probably include an introduction to the shamanic universe such as I give in the next chapter. And you will be asked to think of a starting place, usually somewhere with a route downwards, such as a well, an animal hole or the root of a tree. Some teachers ask you to imagine such a place. I always ask that you think of a place that you actually know. After all, you are not only going to start from this place but you are going to return to it later. Do you really want to return from the spirit realms to a place that exists only in your imagination?

You are most likely to be asked to lie down and cover your eyes with a scarf. Although some native shamans, like those from Tuva or Mongolia, stand and dance while they Journey, lying down is both more common and easier for beginners. To someone watching, this is probably all they would see – a roomful of people lying down, eyes covered, listening to a steady drumbeat. Your body stays in this world as your soul undertakes its Journey.

Led by the rhythmic noise of a drum, you go, in your imagination, to your starting place and begin to descend. Don't be concerned about using your imagination. It is a useful tool. At some stage, and don't worry about when this happens, the Journey will take over. You are in a tunnel. Maybe the tunnel is through earth, with tiny white roots sticking out through the tunnel walls. Maybe it is rocky and you begin to wish that you'd had some experience of caving to help you. Maybe it is lined with books and pictures like Alice in Wonderland's. Every tunnel is different. But what they have in common is that at the end is the Lower World.

I will tell you more about the Lower, the Middle and the Upper Worlds in the next chapter. For now, you simply explore the place. And, sooner or later, because this is what you have come for, you meet an animal. Your animal. A spirit that is your power animal helper. An animal that loves you.

Later in the workshop you might make a Journey to the Upper World and meet a Teacher. You may visit the Middle World. I hope you will do some dancing and rattling because the spirits seem to love dancing and rattling. And I hope that your workshop teacher says something to you about being well grounded before you leave. I don't want you driving your car into a ditch on the way home!

CHAPTER TWO
···································

THE SHAMANIC UNIVERSE

In his book, *Shamanism, Archaic Techniques of Ecstasy*, Eliade wrote, *'The Shaman specialises in a trance during which his soul is believed to leave his body and ascend to the sky or descend to the underworld.'*

All over the world the shaman's view of the spiritual structure of the universe is remarkably similar. There is the Middle World, in which we live, there is the Upper World, which is found by travelling into the sky, and there is the Lower World beneath the ground. In any of these worlds the shaman is able to communicate with the spirits who live there. The three worlds are linked, in many parts of the world, by a great tree. Although to people living in a modern, materialist culture, these experiences are often termed 'superstition' or 'imagination', to shamans in a trance state they are very real.

Many shamans reach the Upper World by climbing this tree or rising on the smoke of a fire. The Lower World is often entered by following the roots of a tree or by going through an animal hole, rather like Alice on her way to Wonderland, although I remember one student who simply sank through the ground from wherever she was in this reality. Many peoples believe that the Upper and Lower Worlds are themselves divided into several different layers. For example, in some Siberian hunting cultures there might be three different levels in the Upper World, while in other areas there might well be nine, twelve or more levels.

Shamans trained in shamanic societies are taught what to expect when they set out on a Journey. We do not have that structure. Most of us had never heard of the different levels of reality before we attended our first shamanic workshop. Maybe that is why, on a typical introductory workshop, everyone's Upper and Lower Worlds are so different. This is one of the ways in which shamanism in our culture is unlike that in many native societies. Of course, many centuries ago, when the culture of these islands was still shamanic, we had our native versions of the three levels. Maybe the best known here are the nine worlds of the Norse myths, divided between three levels and joined by the World Tree, Yggdrasil, and the Heaven and Hell of the Christian traditions.

Usually we find, on workshops, that students' Lower Worlds are landscapes of some kind that echo (or are echoed in) our own world of Ordinary Reality. There are areas, in my Lower World, of flat grassland, of mesas (which we tend to associate with the deserts of the southwestern United States but which also occur – albeit, covered in trees – in North Yorkshire) and of coniferous forest. Sea cliffs and beaches are common, so is deciduous woodland or park-land. Human (or human-like) habitation and inhabitants occur, although more rarely than they do in the Upper World.

This is the start of one of my early Journeys:

I landed on a pile of leaves, picked myself up and opened the door [which is always at the bottom of my tunnel]. Outside it was dusk. Immediately in front of me was the stream, which today had stepping stones [sometimes there is a bridge, sometimes it is shallow enough to paddle across. Occasionally it is not there at all]. I crossed and came to the fork in the path. To my left the path snaked across the grasslands to the distant desert with its mesas and buttes. I took the right-hand path, into the woodland. Here the path is raised on a wooden causeway over marshy ground. I passed the area of higher, dry ground where I often meet to talk with my spirits and continued along the path, which left the wet, deciduous woodland and entered the sandy-floored pine forest. Now it was dark and I followed my power animal closely. The path split into three. To the left is the Round House. Ahead are the Caves. I took the right-hand path, which leads to my Teacher's house.

According to several writers on shamanism, the Lower World can be full of menace and dangers, a place polluted by demons and ghosts.

I have even come across shamanic practitioners who refuse to Journey in the Lower World because they believe it to be evil.

I must say that this is not my experience, nor is it that of our students, although, of course, that notion is there in our traditions, whether it is the Christian Hell that we expect to find or Niflheim, the Norse land of the dead. But, on the whole, people who come on shamanic workshops do not hold unswervingly to such a mental map. We make the first Journey of the introductory workshop to the Lower World to meet a power animal and to reassure ourselves that it is a safe and friendly place. If we had a world-view that said the Lower World was a place of punishment and fire, as the medieval Christians believed, then that would form part of our intention and that fiery place is what we would find, because that is where we would be asking our spirits to conduct us. It would be like having a street map of a city that had only a few places filled in and the rest left blank – we would only be able to find our way to those filled-in places. But here we don't have a map and so we explore wherever our spirits decide to take us. When we say that our intention is to visit the Lower World we are giving our spirits instructions as to where to take us.

I should say something about my use of the word 'intention' here. The 'intention' is the instructions that we give our spirits and ourselves when we undertake a trance Journey.

We might say, 'I am Journeying to ask my spirits for help with my relationship with my mother,' or, 'I am going to meet a spirit who will give me a teaching about compassion.'

Whatever the intention is, it structures the Journey, gives it definition and boundaries. To Journey without an intention is ungrounded and undisciplined. You might get an answer, but how will you know what the question was? It doesn't have to be heavy. It's quite possible for your intention to be: 'To chill out with my spirits and enjoy their company.'

It is worthwhile spending a little time considering the wording of an intention. Graham had had a particularly confusing Journey that I was finding difficult to help him with. I asked him what his intention had been.

He replied, 'To ask what is wrong with my back and what I should do with the rest of my life.'

I would advise you to stick to one main question in your intention. Any other questions should be related to that main one. 'To ask what is wrong with my back and what I can do about it,' would have been fine. 'What should I do with the rest of my life?' is a huge question, requiring a huge answer with many ramifications, conditions and possible outcomes. Maybe it would have been better to ask, in a separate Journey, something along the lines of 'What is my next step on my life's path?'

Sometimes we find that the Upper World, as well as the Lower World, has familiar countryside. But often we discover a much more alien landscape. The part of the Upper World that you visit might be clouds, stretching out on all sides and bouncy to walk upon. Or it may be separate lands, each on a piece of floating rock, joined by ropes and bridges. Or maybe an island in a great sea. All these areas exist in the Upper World and many others, besides.

The Yakut shamans of Siberia visit a place where the people have human bodies and raven heads and where the buildings are made of iron. Although the Upper World is accessed by climbing the World Tree in many parts of Siberia, entering by a hole near the Pole Star is also common. Here we tend to use trees, as well, with a tree that we know standing in for the World Tree. Or we may ascend in the smoke of a fire, as many North American peoples do. When I first started Journeying I used to climb a mountain that I knew well, in Cumbria, and used a cave to reach the Lower World. I often use a tree to go up and an animal hole to descend.

Of course, much of the shaman's work is in what we call the Middle World. This is the world that we know around us, seen through shamanic consciousness. In this world the traditional shaman might go into the forest to rescue someone's soul from the demons who live there, or negotiate with animals, persuading them to offer themselves in the hunt, or to speak with the spirits of the plants that grow in the locality, asking for their help in healing. We don't usually hunt for our food, nor are we generally aware of demons in the forest (which isn't to say that they are not there). But I do a lot of talking to plants, asking for their help, but also asking what conditions my herbs would like in the garden, or how I can help my house plants to survive.

Christine's mother, Mary, was a gifted gardener. She had a particularly fine Christmas cactus, which she loved. Every year it was covered in deep pink blooms. When she became ill and had to go into a nursing home, Christine and I took the cactus to look after. It did not thrive, no matter what we did. It never flowered again. After Mary died it became more and more ill. I decided to Journey to ask what I could do for it.

The spirit of the cactus looked ill and faded. It also looked grief-stricken.

'I want to be with Mary,' it said. 'She's gone and now it is my time to go. Please, put me on your fire, so that I can go quickly to be with her.'

That is what we did. That evening we burnt the cactus on the sitting-room fire, making a ceremony of farewell as we did so. That cactus is one of the few plants that we have had that have not done well. A pink African violet that was hardly ever out of bloom in the several years that we had it told us that it would be happy and thrive,

'... if you tell me how beautiful I am, every now and again.'

That was not hard to do.

And we may not actually go out and hunt animals for our food, but fishing is common and, around here, so is shooting rabbits and pheasants –both of which are eaten. And then there's all the food in the supermarket. We cannot eat without taking life in some way, be it plant or animal. Within our local drumming and Journeying group we have done much work on how we should honour and respect the food that we eat.

Middle World Journeys are to the spirits of those things we see around us; the trees, the stream, the hills and the buildings. The spirits are everywhere, even if we are unaware of them. Here, in Rosedale, in the middle of the North Yorks Moors National Park, where we live, the spirits have asked for help because industry has resulted in the land here needing much healing, some of which I will mention in a later chapter. But all this work is done in the Middle World, some of it actually out on the moors and in the fields and some at home, visiting the Middle World through the shamanic trance.

As I said, views on the Middle World differ. I have heard that the Middle World is dangerous, even 'polluted' by humans. Equally I have heard that it is a uniformly friendly place and the worst that you can get from a Middle World spirit is 'indifference'. My experience, and that of our friends and students, does not bear out either of these. We have found the Middle World spirits to be like humans in that they have many different reactions to being approached by us. If you go out into the marketplace of a small town and try to befriend every person you come across some will be friendly back. You may meet one with whom you can have a deep and lasting friendship. Many people in the marketplace will have their own concerns and tasks. They have no desire for a relationship with you. And some, through fear, pain, distress or just having got out of bed the wrong side that morning will be downright hostile! We do not have the right to assume that everyone will want out of a relationship the same as we do. Middle World spirits are the same. If we have the intention of meeting a spirit who will help and teach us then that is what our own personal spirits will take us to meet. Equally, if we just go and meet any spirit then we should not be surprised if that spirit is not particularly friendly.

In some parts of the world there is a tendency towards considering the spirits as superior beings and the shaman as the 'slave of the spirits'. In other places we find the opposite view that the shaman is the 'master of the spirits'. From many cultures we can read about battles between shamans in Non-ordinary Reality or about cursing being as big a part of the shaman's repertoire as healing is. These viewpoints have led to accusations by various practitioners that either members of native shamanic societies have got it 'wrong' – assuming that the messages of love, equality and ways to lead an ethical life that we receive are somehow more advanced than those that the native shamans get – or that they have it right and we are doing it wrong. I think the answer to this is in Piers Vitebsky's assertion that, *'I believe that shamans' activities have meaning only in relation to their social context.'* We get the spirits and the ways of working that are best for us, in our culture. Our culture is one that finds it easy to abuse power and hard, sometimes, to recognise love. Therefore, I think, we often attract spirits who are willing to help us work particularly with these issues. We have found that, far from wanting masters or servants, the spirits who work with us and with our students want a partnership – something that I think our culture can only benefit from.

We have already seen that shamans work with the help of their spirits, whether these are animal, human or plant. Without their spirits shamans cannot function. Spirit helpers may carry the shaman on their backs across land, over sea or through the air. Or they may lend their bodies to the shaman so that he or she can experience being a tiger, an oak or a standing stone. Helpers can give warnings, advice or help. They can lend their power so that the shaman can achieve things not otherwise possible. Shamanic tools, such as a drum or a rattle, have their own spirits who lend their aid to a venture. Or they may act as messengers and emissaries for the shaman.

Again, who comes to help and teach us depends a lot on what culture we work in. The Sora shamans of India work with previous shamans who are now dead. During ceremonies it is the previous shaman who officiates. The Sora also have a high-caste Hindu, who lives in the underworld and lends his powers to the shaman.

The relationship between the shaman or shamanic practitioner and his or her animal spirits is subtle and complex. One of our students, Lisa, had some serious mental and emotional problems that she was working through. During the time that she was working on these problems her power animal became sick. Lisa needed the power from her power animal, which gave unstintingly, simply in order to keep going. Gradually, Lisa recovered and is now strong and happy. So is her power animal. All over the world there are different ways of interacting with our spirits.

I've talked a lot about spirits, sometimes about spirit Teachers, sometimes about power animals. You might be confused by now as to which word to use. Don't worry. The spirits don't need to conform to labels and each person's spirits may have different ideas when it comes to what they want to be called.

But, generally, I would use the term 'power animal' or, to make the distinction even clearer, 'primary power animal' for those spirits who, like Lisa's, lend us their power regularly. These spirits are closely linked with us and are in some societies even regarded as part of us. If they are sick or we lose our connection to them, then we become sick and will eventually die. Certainly, I know that mine is always with me. He is sitting on my shoulder as I write this and I am always aware of the connection between us. He has been with me in past lives, as well. We are very close. I often get asked what my power animal is. The subject seems to raise a great deal of curiosity. I don't say what or who my helpers are, because I believe, along with many other shamanic practitioners around the world, that to do so diffuses their power.

Daniel had just completed an introductory workshop and was delighted but slightly embarrassed by his newly met power animal. He was a big man, tall and well built, and his power animal was small, timid and fluffy. He went out with friends the next evening.

'So, what happened at this workshop?' asked his friends.

He told them about his power animal and they had a good laugh at the idea of Daniel with a power animal that he could have enclosed in his hands.

We met Daniel a few weeks later and asked how his shamanic work was going. He became very distressed.

'I can't Journey. I feel disconnected and ill all the time.' Concerned, we asked more questions. Daniel told us about his evening with his friends and, also, about a recent holiday he had spent with his wife, in Scotland. He told us of standing on a bridge, and admiring the stream below, when he had noticed a movement amongst the rocks and saw a this-reality version of his power animal. To his horror, the animal slipped into the water, struggled for a moment then disappeared. He rushed to the stream's edge but was unable to do anything to help the drowning creature. Since that event he had felt the symptoms described above. Christine offered to Journey for him.

I went with my power animals to the Lower World and we began to search for the missing spirit. One of my power animals picked up the scent and we went in pursuit. The small creature was rushing away as fast as it could and was obviously deeply distressed. We caught up with it and stopped its headlong flight. I asked it why it was running away.

It said, 'He doesn't want me. He's ashamed of me. I'm not grand enough for him and he laughs about me with his friends. I'm not coming back. I'm a very private creature and I don't want to be talked about in this irreverent way.'

I said, 'Daniel needs you. He realises that now. Meeting you had overwhelmed him and he didn't know how to handle it, so he reacted, through embarrassment, by belittling himself and you to his friends. He realises that now and really wants you back.'

It shook its head. 'Well, it's too late.'

I asked it, if Daniel promised to honour it, it would agree to come back. Grudgingly it agreed.

Christine broke her Journey in order to ask Daniel if he agreed to honour his power animal. Daniel, in tears, resolved to do so. Christine returned to the spirit, who said:

'Well, all right. I'll come back if he'll light a candle to me every night for a fortnight, if he'll keep a picture of me in a drawer where no one else can see it and if he never, ever tells anyone else about me, ever!'

A spirit Teacher, or Guide, is more often, but not always, to be found in human, or humanoid, form. They have often, again not always, been alive on this earth at some time in the past. If so, then they have achieved great wisdom and compassion by the time they begin to teach us. But they are not perfect. They are still learning. I was doing some shamanic work with a student, Kate. Kate had asked her Teacher for help with something particular and she came back from her Journey looking worried. Her Teacher had told her that he didn't know how to deal with this and that Kate should ask me to ask my Teacher about it.

I Journeyed to my Teacher. She was waiting for me with another of my spirit helpers. She pushed me in the direction of this helper. 'Go and amuse yourselves,' she said.

I went over to my helper and we chatted. As we talked, I saw a young man approach my Teacher. This was Kate's Teacher. The two Teachers talked for a long time and then the young man left. I went over to my Teacher.

'All sorted,' she said. 'He'll be really good when he's learned a bit more.'

I came back to Kate and she Journeyed to ask her Teacher once again. This time he was happy and able to help her. (Incidentally, I use a capital letter for spirit Teachers mainly to differentiate them from Ordinary Reality teachers, such as you might meet on a workshop.)

My own Teacher has, until recently, always appeared as an animal. Now she has begun to appear to me as a woman dressed in the skins of the animal that she was. When I asked her why this was, she replied, 'You don't need to worry about it. It's because of things happening in my spiritual growth, not yours.'

I have two main Teachers, one for general work, often personal growth, but also for dealing with such things as disruptive spirits in houses, and one who helps me with healing. I am very close to both these Teachers, so close that they have let me see their own power animals. The first time I saw them I asked my power animal, 'Do you have a power animal?'

He gave me a 'don't be stupid' look and said, 'I *am* a power animal!'

That was a few years ago and gave me one of my first lessons about the differences between power animals and Teachers.

In addition I have several other Teachers. One I see occasionally. She generally helps me with objects that I need for healing. She gave me the eye that I mention in the chapter on soul retrieval. She has helped me to find shamanic ways to use plant oils and crystals. Interestingly, she is one of two Teachers I have that I know I share with other people.

One Teacher is an old Chinese man. Usually he helps me when I need to talk to ancestor spirits, but we have family in China and when I visit them I naturally speak to Chinese spirits. This Teacher helps me whenever I am dealing with Chinese spirits, whether they are ancestral, local land spirits or anything else where a Chinese perspective might help.

Another Teacher appears only when I have to do work which takes me into or near the Land of the Dead. Then most of my spirit helpers stay back and only this Teacher accompanies me.

On our introductory workshops we send students to meet a spirit Teacher. Usually it is their main Teacher that they meet on this first occasion. Several students come having already done spirit work other than shamanism, and are already in contact with a spirit that they often know as a 'Guide'. Usually they will meet the same entity as a Teacher. It is only the label that differs.

But sometimes they meet someone totally different. This happens when the student has done specialist work, usually healing, with their Guide. If the student carries on with their shamanic training and decides to learn shamanic healing then the first Journey of the healing workshop is to meet a Teacher who will help with shamanic healing work. Often they re-meet their old Guide then.

One of the things that I often do while healing is to bring back an animal to help the client. Sometimes this is a primary power animal but, more often, it is an animal that will help with the recovery from the client's immediate problem. For example, when doing a soul retrieval I almost always bring back an animal at the same time. This animal is usually to assist with the integration of the soul part. And, of course, in shamanic work we meet spirits all the time. Some of these meetings are fleeting and some spirits are ones we are helping or ones that are harming our client or just ones who are passing the time of day. But some will agree to help us and we will form a relationship with these. All these, I would simply term spirit helpers. And, while it is usual to have one, or sometimes two, power animals, you can have any number of spirit helpers – if you go out to find them. Teachers and spirit helpers, on the whole, only work with those people who seek them out. Everyone has a power animal, even if they don't know about it. Without one we could not survive.

Now, I've said that the best way to learn about shamanism, in the UK at least, is to go on a workshop and that this is not a 'how to' book. But I realise that, since you are reading this, you are probably interested in what your own power animal may be. I would suggest that you don't rely on lists which match a power animal to your birth date, or the letters of your name. In my experience the animal that you come up with will not tally with what the spirits may provide. Nor can I advise you to choose an animal that you like for yourself. The choice is up to the spirits.

But many people find themselves conscious of a particular animal that is hanging around, in pictures or ornaments. If you find this happening, then notice what animals you are drawn to, but also be mindful of your own ego needs. Beware of 'romantic' ideas about what animal your spirit should be. Many people say that they are aware of Eagle, Wolf, Bear or Dolphin. Not many people claim to be drawn to Rabbit or to Budgerigar. And yet, when we do that first Journey, it could well be Rabbit or Budgerigar who turn up. Please don't reject – as I have known some people do – your power animal, simply because you are not open to the lessons that that animal can teach you.

Many years ago, when I was doing my first Journey to meet my power animal, someone on the same workshop was meeting his. It was a dog. He told the dog that it was not spiritual enough for him. Everyone else, Journeying in the room at the same time, heard that dog howling.

But many people who do not Journey themselves know what their power animal is. They may have attended an introductory workshop, met the animal and then decided that shamanism was not their path, or they may have had a power animal brought back for them by a shamanic practitioner. If you are one of these people and you know what your animal is, but maybe do not know how to relate to it, here are a few things that you might like to try.

First of all, try dancing with it. Pick a place, indoors or out, where you will not be disturbed. Then rattle and shuffle your feet, inviting the animal to dance with you. Gradually allow your body and the rattle to do whatever they want to do. The spirits really seem to love a good dance. If you haven't got a rattle, use some beans in a jam jar. It works just as well.

Make a small shrine to your animal. Maybe a picture, a candle and a stick of incense. Possibly flowers or a clay model. Go with what feels right. If you are a little embarrassed at the idea of a shrine in your house, where people visiting might look askance, remember that the shrine does not have to be either big or obvious. A post-card of the animal, tacked to the wall beside your desk, for example, will not shout out, 'Here is a shrine!' but you will know what it is and that is the important thing.

A third idea is to have a daily practice of greeting your power animal. Try just saying, 'Hello.' You may already have a daily prayer or meditation. If so, incorporate greeting your animal into any practice that you have. You might want to leave it as something along the lines of, 'Good morning, Blackbird,' or you may like to light a candle or a stick of incense, and sit with Blackbird for a few minutes. If you do not have a daily practice but find that the idea appeals to you, have a look at the suggestion for an 'element meditation' at the end of chapter six.

A common category of spirit helper is that of plants. Shamans all over the world use plants to help them. Many people will have heard of South American shamans using psychotropic plants, which are generally considered not so much as spirit helpers but as powerful and knowledgeable Teachers. But many non-psychotropic plants are used by the shaman as well, and I have several plant spirit helpers that assist me, usually with healing. Most of these are plants that I have met locally, although two of them are ones I met in China. They have many skills. The Chinese ones sing through me when I am getting rid of intrusions from a client's body, singing to the intrusion of the beauty of its true home and persuading it to leave the client. One plant helper sits in my mouth to enable me to suck out intrusions without swallowing them and thereby making myself ill. Others lend their healing help to water for my clients to drink. Your plant spirit helpers may work in other ways. Plants have many talents.

Since one of these talents can be to help the shaman to undertake the trance Journey, this might be a good time to mention some of the various ways that are used around the world for the shaman to enter Non-ordinary Reality. Using psychotropic drugs is probably one of the best known. In the types of societies that use these plants the 'trip' is incidental to the communication with the spirits and the healing or knowledge that is brought back for the community. All too often here I have heard people say that they are 'shamans' because they take hallucinogenic drugs and enjoy the experience. But, if they are not communicating with the spirits in order to manifest some change for the better in their community, they are not practising shamanism. Within traditional societies drugs are used with respect and care, for spiritual reasons only. Our society is one that has lost its relationship with plants and which abuses rather than uses drugs. We use powerful and dangerous things for play.

Similarly we do not have a balanced relationship with food and, therefore, I would not recommend fasting as a way of entering Non-ordinary Reality, although this method is used, in some parts of Asia and North America particularly. Anorexia and bulimia are illnesses of our society, not of shamanic ones. Although the time may come when you personally feel that your contact with your spirits is harmonious and strong enough to try fasting it is not a beginner's technique.

In many places dancing and chanting are used, although usually accompanied by drumming and rattling. While the long, ecstatic dances such as the Ghost Dance are not beginners' dances we do dance with our spirits for many reasons, not least because all the spirits I have ever met seem to really like dancing. I think this is partly because, when you are dancing with your spirits, there is a feeling of great connection with them. Dancing and singing are used in many ways in shamanism, but one important and often dismissed way is to celebrate and enjoy. Our spirits often say to us:

'Just enjoy yourself. Life is to be enjoyed.'

Generally we use sonic driving, a monotonous noise on which we travel to Non-ordinary Reality. In particular we use a drum, which is easy, convenient and safe and which is used all around the world for shamanic Journeying. In the Americas, rattles are commonly used, almost to the extent of replacing the drum in South America, and in parts of Southeast Asia shamans use a winnowing fan, which is swished rhythmically, to enter trance. I have never used a winnowing fan but I often use a rattle, for Journeying, for healing, for dancing. It is particularly useful for use outside where a drum might be cumbersome.

I'd like to mention drumming tapes. I do prefer live drumming and so do most people that I know but most of us also use tapes. There are times when live drumming just isn't possible. A personal stereo means that you can sit under a tree in the park on a sunny day, to Journey, without anyone thinking it odd. And not everyone is lucky enough to have someone to drum for them. You can Journey while drumming yourself but it is more difficult and not always appropriate.

Who, from within a community, becomes a shaman differs around the world. In some areas, for example among the nomadic Sami of northern Scandinavia, every family group is likely to have a shaman, while in, for example, Tuva, in Siberia, only a few will be called. But everywhere, the shaman is called by the spirits and, often, the call is not a welcome one. Shamanic peoples know that the shaman's job is one of danger and hardship. Hunting is traditionally a male activity almost everywhere and most shamans in societies that rely heavily on hunting will be male. In agrarian societies there are more female shamans. In Korea all shamans are either women or, occasionally, men dressed as women. Here, although it is mainly women who attend workshops in the first place, the spirits' call is heard by both sexes equally. Another example of a society getting the shamanism that it needs.

When the shaman has been called, in traditional societies, there follows a period of instruction, often accompanied by an illness, either physical or mental. This illness is seen in several ways. For some it happens because the future shaman is resisting his or her path and the confusion and dilemma brings about the illness. Or it may be that the illness itself is a method for the spirits to teach the potential shaman.

Although in our culture the call to the spirits usually happens *after* a time of instruction rather than before, since people here decide to attend a workshop and any 'becoming a shaman' comes later, if at all, these two categories of illness can clearly be seen amongst shamanic students. I have known people become ill when the spirits have given them a task, such as Daniel was given when he was asked to light a candle to his power animal, and they have not done as was wanted. I don't believe that the spirits actually give us an illness as punishment but going against our soul's path is bound to make us ill. And I have known many people who have found their way to shamanism as a result of trying to find a way to learn whatever lessons their illness has to teach them.

During the education of a shaman – which, let's face it, goes on throughout the shaman's existence – there is a particular experience that happens. Not all shamanic students have this initiatory experience, but when it does happen it marks a definite leap forward in

27

power. Essentially, the shaman is dismembered or stripped to the bone or otherwise destroyed by his or her spirit helpers, and then rebuilt into a new, more powerful, more skilful person. It can be frightening and painful when it happens, but it is part of a shamanic experience that is worldwide. It is also not a 'one-off' experience. I have met people who consider that they have no more need of learning since their dismemberment experience. But these experiences happen when you change enough to need a new spirit body to go with the 'new you'. I have had several. I know I still have much to learn.

Another thing that may happen as you develop as a person who takes shamanic work seriously is that the spirits will give you a 'spirit name' – usually of the 'Running Deer' style, rather than 'Sam'. Some people decide to use their spirit name openly. Others use theirs when they are teaching, healing or otherwise operating as a shamanic practitioner. Many, including myself, keep theirs private. I use it occasionally during Journeying, usually in formal situations where I have to talk to spirits doing a job in Non-ordinary Reality. Very few people in this reality know my spirit name. This way I keep its power.

The student has to keep changing, to keep becoming a new person, and this has to happen in Ordinary Reality as well as in Non-ordinary Reality. When we are serious about our shamanic work we strip ourselves down to the bare bones of our emotional and mental makeup. This may be a distressing process but it is a vital part of our spiritual growth. When we avoid it or put it off we lay ourselves open to this change anyway. I can think of many students who have decided to work only for others and not on themselves who have had the type of illness – for example, a nervous breakdown – which requires us to do this changing in spite of ourselves. I have said that the shaman operates as part of the community, working for that community, and that is so. But without time spent on personal growth as well, even the most knowledgeable shaman will be without power.

I have said that in many shamanic societies the role of the shaman is not one to be envied. The shaman's job is hard and dangerous and it would probably surprise many native shamans that so many people in the British Isles want to learn to be shamans.

Well, maybe it would reassure them to know that very few people come on our workshops with the stated aim of 'becoming a shaman'. Those that do tend to give up quickly when they realise that practising shamanism is hard work, or they change their minds about what they want from the workshop. The vast majority of attendees on an Introductory workshop are curious. They have heard the word 'shamanism' and they want to know what it is. Some of them will leave, curiosity satisfied, and never attend another shamanic workshop. Others will have had their appetites whetted and will go on to further study. Some attendees come because they are alternative or complementary practitioners of one sort or another and want to add shamanic healing to the list.

Most of these people have no thought of becoming a shaman. Eventually, if they continue to work shamanically, they will either learn how to work for others by healing, psychopomping (that is, guiding the souls of the dead to the Land of the Dead), land healing or in other ways, or they will use shamanism solely for their own self-development. This is a valid and very useful way of using shamanism. It doesn't make you a shaman, of course, but working shamanically does seem to push forward spiritual growth faster than anything else that I know of.

If they become interested in helping others with their shamanism then I would call them 'Shamanic Practitioners'. There are many of these up and down the country. Some work simply with shamanism, others blend shamanism with Reiki, crystal healing or some other therapy.

None of this makes them shamans. In fact, there is an argument that shamans do not exist in our society. But I disagree with this.

I feel that, in order for someone to be a shaman, certain criteria need to be fulfilled. First, it has to be shamanism that is practised and not just 'being with nature' or 'playing at Red Indians' or any other of the myriad of activities that goes under the name of 'shamanism'. (I know of someone who classes storytellers and jugglers as shamans. It's a popular word.) Second, there has to be a relationship with the spirits. This may seem self-evident but there are, in fact, many people who are not happy with the idea of understanding the spirits as entities. They prefer to regard the spirits as aspects of their subconscious mind or to view their power animal as a symbol in much the same way as a zodiacal sign.

Third, there has to be the acknowledgement of the spirits that you are a shaman. This comes about eventually for those people who live their shamanism and who are prepared to work deeply on their own issues as well as using their shamanism for helping others. It is not something that is likely to happen unless you know that your contact with your spirits is the most important thing in your life. And it is up to the spirits, not you.

Fourth, there has to be the acknowledgement of the community and the community's use of the shaman's skills. This one is hard in our society, since the word 'shaman' is not in most people's vocabulary. Also, it can be quite hard to define 'community' here. The *Oxford English Dictionary* stresses that members of a community must have something in common. We are used to thinking of that something as being location. The community is the people who live close by and, unless you live in a very unusual place, they are not likely to call you a shaman. Nor, of course, are they likely to have the same world-view of spirits as someone in a shamanic culture does. But they might well understand that you can help them in some way, and be prepared to seek out that help. Also, to a large extent, here we can understand 'community' to mean friendship groups, groups of like-minded people. And there are groups (for example shamanic drumming groups) which understand the concepts of shamanism and whose members are happy to go to those members that they regard as 'shamans' for healing, spiritual guidance or other shamanic help.

And fifth, the 'treatment' has to work! In Tuva, even though the Soviet Union no longer rules, there is a lot of Soviet-style bureaucracy. Shamans carry cards, stating that they are shamans. But even so, the standard way of deciding who is and who is not a shaman is the age-old one, found in shamanic cultures everywhere, of seeing if the patients get better. It seems to me that this is a valid test here, as well.

CHAPTER THREE

SHAMANIC HEALING

Throughout the world and throughout history shamans have under-taken many tasks for their communities. It has been suggested that, in hunting societies, the goal of obtaining animals for the hunt is more fundamental to the wellbeing of the society than is healing the sick. Some shamans specialise in divination and some in rituals and cere-monies. And in many cultures the shaman is not the only, or even the primary, healer. There may be, within the society, men and women whom we tend to call medicine people or witch doctors, healers and communicators with spirits who do not necessarily undertake the shamanic Journey. There may well be herbalists. There could be priests and monks who heal using prayer or spells. Healing, even in so-called primitive societies, is not the sole preserve of the shaman.

But shamanic healing is a large part of the work of most modern shamanic practitioners and shamans, whether they live here, in the UK, or in some small clan still practising traditional methods. And this is largely because healing is where the demand is.

Trudi was referred to us by her hypnotherapist.

'Can you help her?' he said. 'I have her here. Will you talk to her?'

I said that I was willing to try and she came onto the telephone. She was clearly in distress and gradually her story came out.

She had spent years in therapy of one sort or another – psychother-apy, past-life therapy and, most recently, hypnotherapy. The result of all of these had been the same. Trudi, like me, believes in reincarnation. Indeed, although not all native peoples do, I have never spoken to a spirit who did not simply take the fact of reincarnation for granted. In her last life Trudi had died in the 1940s. She was at that time a man, aged about thirty-five, who had died convinced that he had caused the deaths of many men and women. During her first therapy session Trudi had discovered this man in an underground cave, filthy and ragged, huddled in a corner surrounded by the skeletons of those he believed he had killed. Over three years of therapy she had tried, as she said, '... to bring him out of the cave. But he won't come.'

Using guided visualisations and hypnotism Trudi had brought him to the surface over and over again. But, every time, when she went to check on him, he was back in his cave huddled amongst the bones.

She was at her wits' end. Her therapists were no better off.

'Has it always been you that has gone to help him?' I asked.

'How else?'

I tried to explain. 'Have any of your therapists gone to speak to him on your behalf?' I don't know what is possible in these therapies.

'No,' she said.

'Have you asked him why he will not come out?'

'He won't speak to me.'

I asked a final question. 'If you succeed in getting him out what will you do then?'

Trudi didn't understand. I elaborated.

'Even if he is out of this cave, he and you will still be separate. That's not really what you want, is it?'

She agreed but had obviously not thought any further than 'getting him out'. She made an appointment and we said goodbye.

She arrived about a week later. Over coffee Trudi told Christine all that she had previously told me. In some ways the case was a simple soul retrieval – a part of Trudi was missing. It needed to be brought back. The situation was complicated only by the fact that the missing part was dead. We did the soul retrieval, got some information from our spirits about how Trudi should best work to integrate the soul part and went back downstairs for another coffee. Trudi has needed no further work doing. I am convinced that part of the reason that we succeeded when other therapists had failed is that we took the story at face value, as Trudi did herself. The man in the cave was part of Trudi, but a part that was separated from her and lost. The healing was a matter of healing him as well and then reuniting the two parts to make a whole Trudi. We did not view the man as a part of Trudi's psyche, or as a construct of her subconscious mind.

There are many ways of healing in this world, beautiful ways practised by sincere, wonderful people. Ways like Reiki or spiritual healing. They have results. On occasions, stunning results. We live in a beautiful and loving universe and if we, genuinely, with intention, ask it for healing, for ourselves or for others, healing will come. But sometimes healing energy is not all that is needed. Sometimes something has gone seriously wrong on the spiritual level – whether as a result, or as a cause, of trauma. Trudi had suffered soul loss, where part of the soul leaves because, for some reason – in this case, guilt – something happens that that part cannot cope with. Trudi's situation was complicated by the fact that the soul part had been lost in a previous life. The soul is very resilient and, although there would eventually come a point when someone had lost too much soul to incarnate at all, most of us can cope with a few missing parts. Soul retrieval is a large part of the work of any shamanic practitioner and I shall say more about it in the next chapter. It is probably the best known aspect of shamanic healing. But it is not the only aspect. Many things can go wrong on a spiritual level and when this happens the problem can manifest as a physical problem, or a mental or emotional one.

Healings are necessary because, at some stage, by actions, thoughts or lifestyles the client has drawn the soul loss or the intrusion to him- or herself. Such treatment as soul retrievals or extractions, where the shaman takes out something that is in the client that should not be, may be enough to heal. But, more likely, changes will be needed in the client's attitude towards him- or herself and surroundings in order to prevent the illness continuing and more soul loss occurring.

I am not inferring blame here. We are products of many influences and can only overcome them in our own time, which may or may not concur with the timetable of a therapist. But there is a great freedom in taking not blame but responsibility for our own wellness. We can only change ourselves, we cannot change others. If we wait for another person to change, or for our lives to change without effort from ourselves, we will be waiting for a very long time!

Help will be there from the spirits when we are ready to ask for it. But we have to ask and we have to be willing to make necessary changes in order to be well. Then we can take control of our lives and the way in which we lead them.

When we are ill, in whatever way that manifests, whether we are needing help physically, mentally or emotionally, it is always because something spiritually is wrong. If we are well, balanced, full of our own power, then nothing major will go wrong. I say major because it is the job of our power animals to keep us from harm, not to keep us from the incidents that will help us to learn our life's lessons.

When something is wrong spiritually then everything in our life, including illnesses, fears, addictions and phobias, is pointing out to us our need to change. From our own soul's point of view even such a devastating thing as a cancer is a very small happening, a thing of one lifetime out of many and important mainly for its gift of itself as a signpost for us. To become truly well we must let go of the need for such signposts and travel beyond them. And that means inviting change into our lives.

We must be sure that we want it. If our uncertainty has let in an intrusion that has more lust for life than we have then our intention to be well will be weak.

If our illness, be it fear or virus, is more alive than we are, has more love of life than we have, then its intention to live will be stronger than ours and it will survive at our expense.

All our healing techniques are just that. Techniques. Only love can heal. And the Universe is full of love. But we cannot heal if for any reason we shut ourselves off from that love. Or mistake it and think we have love when, in reality, we have sentimentality or possession.

Love is not an easy thing. Nor is it in any way wishy-washy. But it is necessary for healing. To be well you have to love yourself. To heal others you have to love them. And neither one of these is possible without the other.

Love is a hard thing to define. It's easier to talk in metaphor and poetry about it. And easier to say what it isn't. I hear the phrase 'unconditional love' often and it always puzzles me slightly. Isn't it a tautology? Can there be such a thing as 'conditional love'?

My thinking at the moment about this is that love needs three things in order for it to be more than just a word. It needs compassion. It needs truth or integrity. And it needs intention, focus, clear thinking.

Within that love we are connected to the spirits, to each other and to the land. We are all connected. Sometimes we lose sight of that fact and then we begin to act in a way of separation. But separation is an illusion, albeit an illusion that we often find easy to believe. All that has fallen away is our awareness of our connection. We are not separate. All that we do affects everything else, for good or ill. We are all connected to the Web.

My pain is your pain and your joy is my joy. I cannot be whole while you are dis-membered. This is not only empathy – 'I feel for you' – but literal truth. If you are sick, being connected to the great Web of Life that includes all things, then the entire universe is that little bit more sick. I am connected to that Web and therefore I am that much more sick also. And if you are well, likewise.

It is, therefore, in my best interests to help you see the possibility of wellness. Not to 'make you well' for that would take your power and, in our connection, would dis-empower me also, but to try to act as a signpost towards a possible well-ness and to give every assistance that is asked for.

The intention of the Universe is Love. We can feel that love in our most ecstatic experiences. Indeed, this is a way that we define ecstasy. Therefore, being connected to the Universe, all we do with love will have stronger intention and more power than all we do without love. With love we are working *with* the Universe, not against it.

But, as with many walks of life, love, alone, is not enough. When things go wrong, spiritually as well as in more tangible ways, we need to know how to set them right. Often, when there is need for shamanic healing one of two things has happened. Either something that belongs in you has gone or something that belongs elsewhere has come into you. Of the things you are most likely to lose, soul is the most serious and I will say more about soul loss and retrieval in the next chapter. We lose power easily, too, usually by giving it away. I'm sure that we can all think of instances where we have given our power to someone else, not because we wanted to but because, at that moment, we could not think of anything else to do.

Power retrieval is probably one of the most useful and wonderful things that can be done for another person.

Harry was ten. His mother had brought him to me because he had an ear infection that would not clear up. I Journeyed to ask my spirits what I should do.

'An extraction,' my healing Teacher said, 'and a power retrieval.'

I asked Harry's mother to drum for me and prepared myself for the healing. 'Don't wear your robe or shout for us,' my Teacher said. 'This once we'll come without that. We don't want to scare Harry.' I asked my spirits to come, whispering to them and beckoning, rather than shouting and whistling as I usually do. (I can't whistle in Ordinary Reality.) Then I took out the intrusion.

I said to Harry, 'Harry, I'm going to lie down here beside you and hold your hand. Then I'm going to ask my spirits to help me find a power animal for you, who will live inside you and help you.'

Harry had just read a fictional book by the children's author Philip Pullman, which deals with creatures that are very like power animals, so Harry was happy with this idea. I lay down and his mother began to drum again.

I began to descend to my Lower World and then, when my spirits signalled to me, I side-stepped into Harry's Lower World. I found myself on a seashore, beneath a beautiful tropical sky. The sea was blue and the beach was of golden sand. The sun shone. Out to sea I could see dolphins playing. I waited and watched, and eventually one of the dolphins separated from the rest and came close into the shore.

'Are you Harry's power animal?' I asked.

It nodded and I asked, 'Will you come back to him, with me?'

Again it nodded and leaped from the sea into my arms. I held it carefully in my hands and it settled into a size that I could manage. I came back to the room and, still holding the dolphin, which I could feel even though, in Ordinary Reality, I couldn't see it, knelt up. I blew through my hands into Harry's chest, blowing the dolphin into him.

This is a fairly standard power retrieval. Harry had had his power returned to him and went away, feeling very pleased at the idea of a dolphin to help him. The ear infection had cleared completely when he returned to the doctor the following day.

Within this account I mention my robe. Not all shamanic practitioners wear a robe, although most that I know will wear something significant while they are healing. It might be a special necklace or a particular shirt. My robe is black and covered with things – mirrors, feathers, shells, bells and beads – that my spirits have given me or instructed me to find. Like my other tools, for example my drum or my rattle, the robe itself has a spirit that helps with healing. The items on it lend me their spirits' power also. For example, the mirrors help to turn away anything, such as the spirit of an illness, that I might be taking from a client and do not want to lodge in me. And the very act of putting on the robe helps to get me into the right frame of mind for shamanic work. Look at pictures of shamans from around the world. They almost always wear a robe of some sort.

I also did an extraction for Harry. When we lose something it leaves a space. It is easy for something to find its way in. Indeed, if the space is left for long enough, it is almost inevitable that something will.

The vast majority of these 'things' do not 'possess' us, although such is the media hype, from scare stories in certain magazines to Hollywood films, that most people who feel that there is something in them that shouldn't be tend to assume that it is either a ghost or a demon. It is possible for sensitive people to detect that they hold something 'wrong' inside them. But most of us are so unsure of how we feel when we are fully well that we are not likely to notice the difference. Many intrusions are lost spirits – and I am not talking here of just people's spirits. Although other souls can intrude in this way it is rare. Far more common is that one of the myriad of spirits that inhabit the universe has simply wandered in and has been unable to find its way out. Others have been attracted by the vibrations that those aspects of your life that you should change are giving off.

Remember that I am talking here about the spiritual aspect of an illness. These are spirit entities that have come in and that the shaman can get rid of, not physical things such as cancers. This is a subtle distinction. The presence of an intrusion might *cause* a cancer.

Even more likely is that whatever you need to change in your life, which has allowed the cancer to grow, has also allowed the intrusion to enter. We are used to thinking of health and illness as only physical occurrences. Even the idea of a mental illness other than the all-encompassing 'lunacy' is only a couple of hundred years old and the taking-seriously of emotional ill-health still has a long way to go, as can be witnessed by many who have suffered from stress. It might be useful to consider that although this is so in our culture, for many people around the world the spiritual cause of an illness is the most important aspect. Maybe 'illness' is the wrong word. We tend to focus upon illness because it is one of the more obvious things that goes wrong with us. And, because we tend to think of ourselves as individuals first and part of a community later – if at all – illnesses are what we seek help for. But it is the shaman's job to heal whatever has gone wrong in the community, whether that is physical illness, problems with hunting sufficient food – and if you think that problem doesn't affect us, just try looking at the fishing situation in the North Atlantic and North Sea – finding a reason for floods – again, very topical – or anything else that needs rectifying.

And when it comes to that healing, again we like to think of ourselves as individuals, not-connected, whereas many native societies realise that if the problem is the community's, then the solution has to be the community's also.

We are a long way from that. And yet, every little helps. For Harry's mother, drumming for my Journey to help her son brought her into the healing process and made her a part of it.

Maria needed some work doing. She is a student and a member of our Drumming Group. But, partly because she lives in a remote area and partly because she is, by nature, reclusive, she did not attend very often. Maria had been a Pagan for most of her adult life and, like many to whom Paganism appeals, considered herself to be a 'solitary' practitioner. My spirits felt that this was a large part of Maria's problem. She asked me for help and, on the advice of my spirits and with Maria's permission, I asked the rest of the Drumming Group to help. In this way the Drumming Group is Maria's community and taking the part that other villagers would take in a shamanic society. We fixed a time that we could all attend and I did the extraction and power retrieval that Maria needed, supported by her friends and their spirits. This helped me on a practical level – I had plenty of drummers and rattlers, and someone to open the door for me when I had my hands full of intrusion – but also, and in many ways more importantly, it helped me on a spiritual level, since the room was full of spirits all focused on loving and healing Maria. It helped Maria, of course. She saw that she was part of a community that cared for her and the connection that began to grow then has become ever stronger. And the others who took part were helped by the enormous sense of connection between us all.

I am often asked why I do healings for others. Doesn't this disempower them? Wouldn't it be better if they did their own extractions, maybe with guided visualisation? The question always surprises me slightly because, although I know that there is a 'New Age' feeling that everyone can heal themselves, I don't know anyone who would advocate filling and drilling his or her own teeth, rather than going to the dentist. There is a danger in being too self-sufficient and that is when we become ever more isolated from others. Apart from the practical considerations of the difficulties of taking out intrusions from your own body, why would you want to be so separate? Many people complain that there is no 'community' any more. Well, maybe the word no longer means the same as it did. 'Community' does not often mean the people who live in your village any more. But we have friends, we have groups of like-minded people. 'Community' is what we make it. And we can't have it if we continually try to isolate ourselves. I often read the phrase 'we can each be our own shaman'. If it means we can each have that connection to spirit and the spirits then, yes, I agree. But if it means that we can heal ourselves with no help from others then, no. Not even native shamans are 'their own shamans'. If they are ill, they go to another shaman for healing.

I am convinced that the connection with others who care enough about us to want to help heal us is an essential part of that healing.

Another point is that when you are ill you are low in power. You are then likely not to have enough power to heal, just at the time when you need it most.

I am not suggesting that we passively allow others to take all responsibility for our healing. As I said before, if we want to be well, then we must take responsibility for making the changes in ourselves and our lives that will allow wellness to flourish. The dentist can fill your teeth. She can't come around twice a day to clean them for you. Nor can she get you into her chair without your active effort to be there. Your wellness is your responsibility. Just don't try to do it all alone.

I was talking earlier about intrusions. When the shaman gets rid of the intrusion it is called an 'extraction'. So, what is likely to happen if you go to a shaman for an extraction? Well, there are basically four ways to do an extraction. The first, and the simplest, is by persuading the intrusion to leave of its own accord. This works most often with the kind of intrusion that has become lost, wandered in and decided to stay because it is warm and comfortable. I have spirit helpers who, in these circumstances, will sing through me of the true home of the intrusion and of why it should not stay where it is. Often this will persuade the intrusion to come close to the surface where my spirit helpers can get hold of it and take it back to wherever it belongs.

Another, similar way is to coax the intrusion into an object, a stone, a shell or something else. I use a stone. I sing and coax and – rarely – threaten the intrusion into the stone. Once it is in, I put the stone into a bowl of water. Later, when the treatment is over, I pour both water and stone onto the grass outside. From here my spirit helpers will ensure that it gets back to its true home.

More spectacularly, certainly more noisily, is an extraction done by pulling at the intrusion with your hands. When the intrusion comes near to the surface the shaman grabs it firmly and then, usually with a great shout, flings it away. In many parts of North America the shaman will throw the intrusion towards the nearest large body of water – the ocean, a lake or a river. In Siberia, intrusions are often thrown on to a fire. I throw mine out of the door or window, where one of my spirit helpers waits to grab them and take them away. Once I forgot to open the window. There was a glass crystal hanging in the window and, when I threw the intrusion, from the other side of the room, the crystal swung against the window with such force that the thread snapped, the crystal broke and the window was scratched. Although these intrusions are easier to detect in Non-ordinary Reality they have an effect in Ordinary Reality also. Don't underestimate these entities. They are not psychological constructs of our subconscious mind. I have never since forgotten to open the window!

Another way of getting the intrusion out is to suck. This is, for some reason, considered glamorous. Let me assure you, it is not. It is the part of shamanic healing that I find most unpleasant. The intrusion is sucked out of the client, usually through a tube, and then spat into a bowl of water, sand or salt. This is not particularly pleasant for the client either, if the shaman is retching into a bowl next to them. Still, it is the best way I know of for getting out certain intrusions and for clearing away the general gunge that intrusions often leave behind.

There are precautions to be taken with all these methods. Please do not try them without having been taught first. Extractions can be dangerous, not only for the client, for whom you won't do any good if you leave bits of intrusion in him or her, but also for the practitioner. It is possible for the intrusion to lodge in the shaman. It is not uncommon for healers of many kinds to die young, often of cancers. Let's not invite such things by careless work.

In some societies shamans take the illness into themselves and, over the next week or few weeks or months, transmute the illness inside them. While this is going on the shaman is ill. This has only ever been a minority way of working when viewed worldwide. There seems to be something about it that appeals to many people here – a notion of suffering for others that I think we get from the Christian idea of a saviour taking on our 'sins'. Remember, if you work like this – and you must only do so if your spirits tell you to, for I certainly won't tell you to – and if you mess it up, you will remain ill yourself. Please remember what I said about healers making themselves sick. If you are drawn to this work then please make sure you are not drawn to it because it seems to be glamorous.

The idea that something that does not belong is inside you can be very frightening. But it is a known occurrence in shamanic cultures worldwide. I am always very careful to explain to clients what is going to happen and to tell them not to be disturbed. With the shouting and, particularly if it is a sucking extraction, other noises, this work can be very alarming to someone new to shamanic healing. I am also very careful as to what I tell the client that I have taken out of them. Although the intrusion might look to me like (for example) a slug or snake I usually just say that I took out something that was making them ill. Unless they are shamanically experienced themselves they are not likely to be happy at the idea of a 'creepy-crawly' inside them.

Sometimes the intrusion is something more personal and the client will benefit from knowing about it. Sonia came to me to ask me to help her get over childhood traumas that had included a very difficult relationship with her mother who had suffered from mental illness. When people are mentally ill, I have found that they often throw off parts of their souls. These parts can become intrusions for someone else. There are few cultures that believe we have only one soul. Most believe that there are at least two souls – the body soul and the free soul. The Yagua of the Amazon believe that a person has two souls when alive, but five when dead, the last three only becoming active on death. In the Celebes, the Wana believe that a soul resides in the liver. This is important since they believe there live, in the forest, liver-devouring demons who can steal a person's soul. The Inuit in Greenland believe that every bit of the body, each individual body part has a soul. If a bit is lost, for example in an accident, what happens to the spirit of that part? If a tooth is removed the shaman can bring back the soul of the tooth. This could be very important in the case of an amputation, a hysterectomy or a heart transplant. If that is so, what about the soul of the hair that you have had cut? Your nail parings?

I don't know the answers to all these questions. I know the thought that every time I have my hair cut I am losing soul is dreadful. No doubt Samson felt the same. I also know that if I Journey to nail parings I find that they *have* souls, souls with which I can converse. But I've never had to treat anyone who had problems because of losing hair or nail parings. Or, indeed, teeth. Souls – or, if you are happier with the concept of only one soul per person, soul parts – go missing because you suffer a trauma. Part of you cannot cope with a particular situation – let us say, for example, a road accident – and that part leaves. It is a situation that has evolved for our survival, since had that part stayed you might have died. Instead you live, but with only part of your soul. And you are glad to be alive but you think, 'I've never felt *really* well since the accident', or, 'I feel disconnected from life.'

Sonia's mother had flung off parts of her soul and these had lodged in Sonia. Sonia understood, on some level, when I told her that she had part of her mother. It often happens that what is soul loss for one person becomes an intrusion for another person. I'm sure that you can see how this could happen. If, maybe, a couple were splitting up after a love affair, and each party gave away, however unintentionally, a part of soul to the other party, then what would be soul loss to one would be an intrusion to the other, and vice versa. So, Sonia's mother's soul loss was Sonia's intrusion. And the piece of Sonia's mother had come in with such force that it had dislodged part of Sonia's soul. I consulted my spirits.

I rattled to the four directions, calling in my spirits and my healing Teacher. Then I rattled over Sonia.

'This is Sonia, who needs our help,' I said, introducing her to my spirits. Then I knelt beside her to rattle over her. I have a good relationship with the spirits of my rattles and they soon indicated to me, by changing their note and singing to me, where the intrusion was lodged. My Teacher confirmed the place.

'Here, see,' she said, pointing. 'There is a huge intrusion here.'

I looked and could see a solid lump of what looked like metal. This is unusual. Intrusions usually appear to me in the form of animals, usually invertebrates, reptiles or amphibians. This is common worldwide. However, the lump of 'metal' was clearly not supposed to be in Sonia, and that is what really defines an intrusion. I started to rattle over it. I sang and whistled for a long time and gradually I was aware that the intrusion was moving. Curiosity was bringing it to the surface to find out what was going on.

'Now!' said my Teacher, and I grabbed the intrusion and flung it out of the (open) window, with a great shout. Outside I could see my spirit helper grip it with his talons and then fly off with it. My hands were hot with the heat from the intrusion. I plunged them into a bowl

of cold water that I had by my side, then I came back to look at Sonia.

The hole left by the intrusion was dirty. The intrusion had been there for over thirty years. It was bound to be dirty. I placed my stone on Sonia's chest and began once more to rattle and sing. Gradually the dirt flowed into the stone. When I had got as much as I could I removed the stone and dropped it into another bowl of water.

I lit some incense, made from plants from my garden, with which I have a close friendship, and blew the smoke into the cavity left by the intrusion. Then I sprinkled water into it and had another look. The space was clean, fit for Sonia's missing soul part to come back to.

I set off to look for the missing soul part. When I found it I discovered that the soul part also had an intrusion, another piece of Sonia's mother. I took her to my Teacher's house where my Teacher laid her on the table and asked me to drum while she did this extraction. She took a bird's claw and split open the soul part's chest cavity. Then she asked her spirit helpers to enter the cavity and pass her out the piece of Sonia's mother. They did this and my spirit helper, who already had the first piece, took care of this piece also. Then my Teacher's spirit helpers ate out all the dirt that the intrusion had left. Finally the helpers came out of the cavity and my Teacher sewed the soul part up with strong, neat stitches. Then she handed me the soul part, I put it in my crystal, my soul carrier, and brought it back to Sonia. I knelt beside her and blew the soul part into her.

But I was not yet finished. The two parts needed returning to Sonia's mother, who had died several years previously. I did not expect her to have managed to get to the Land of the Dead with so much soul missing and, sure enough, she was lost in a grey, misty place. She was not really aware of what was happening until I blew the soul parts into her. Then she stretched, stood up and said, 'My goodness! I do feel better!'

I took her to the entrance to the Land of the Dead, where she was greeted and taken in.

I said that intrusions are often attracted to us by the vibrations that those aspects of our lives that need changing are giving off. Petra was deeply unhappy. She spoke of self-hatred, of feeling fear and of being judged. She felt alienated and felt herself to be a victim – a role she did not want for herself. Additionally she had a severe stammer and a constant feeling in her throat that she was going to be sick. I Journeyed to ask my Teacher what to do.

My Teacher said that the stammer was caused by an intrusion in Petra's throat. It had been there a long time and was very comfortable, since Petra was nurturing it through her feelings of alienation and fear. But, of course, Petra could not let go of those feelings while the intrusion was there, feeding on her. I tried to persuade the intrusion out.

'No, I'm staying. Why should I come out when I'm comfortable here? It's warm and cosy and there's plenty to eat.'

I was intrigued.

'What do you eat?' I asked.

'Fear,' it said. 'Anxiety. Self-doubt.'

My Teacher told me to be firmer, and to be ready to grab it when it came to the surface. I began to grumble at it. Then I threatened it. Finally I began to insult it. Then, as it came near to the surface in order to retaliate, I grabbed hold hard and hung on as it fought back. It had many tentacles and tried to wrap them around my arms. I was determined, however, and held it out of the window where my spirit helper could get a good grip and fly away with it.

I cleansed the space that it had left and Journeyed for a power animal for Petra. A condor came and offered to work with her.

He said, 'I will help her to soar above the ground, high enough to see that everything is connected. This will help her to rid herself of the alienation that attracted the intrusion in the first place. If she will work with me to love herself as much as I love her, then she will be well.'

As you can see, this was not an instant cure. Petra continued to stammer until she had learned, with the condor's help, to view herself more kindly. But the sick feeling in her throat disappeared at once. Petra could Journey and so was able to visit her power animal in order to work with him. It is more usual for me to Journey on the client's behalf, since most of my clients do not Journey, to find out what things in his or her life need to change for the 'cure' to make a lasting difference.

I had been interested in what the intrusion ate. I have come across others that lived on fear. And there is plenty of fear around to feed them. I think spirits like this are maybe the psychic equivalent of maggots or dung beetles, the creatures I tend to think of as 'the clean-up crew', without whom we would be knee-deep in waste. It's not surprising that, if such a creature found an ample source of sustenance, it would stay where the food was plentiful.

Petra's feeling of alienation, her sense of lack of connection, is so common. Many of us lead our lives in ways that make us feel alone. We are never alone. We all have a power animal, even if we have never met it, and we all are connected to everything else, to every other spirit in the Universe. But, as I say, we can *feel* alone. And we cannot be well and happy while we feel so disconnected.

I have mentioned that my power animal takes an intrusion back to wherever it belongs. Unless the intrusion is a part of someone else, that is usually all that I need to know and do. But it is important that *something* is done with the intrusion. I heard, recently, of work being done for a client whose intrusion was what we call an attachment – that is, a soul of someone who has died and who, instead of continuing to the Land of the Dead, has attached him- or herself to a living person. The soul had been persuaded to leave the client but had not then been taken onwards to the Land of the Dead. The client made a full recovery, but a few months later, the building was getting a reputation for being haunted, as the poor, lost soul wandered the corridors, opening doors to other therapists' rooms and looking for someone to help it.

In some parts of the world the intrusion is persuaded out of the client and into an animal. This isn't suitable to our culture where a client is not going to thank you for curing her, but killing her cat! Again, I've heard of this happening by accident, when the shamanic practitioner has been careless. On one occasion I know of the client got better but his dog, almost immediately, had a fit and died. A responsible practitioner will make certain that the intrusion is taken care of. A lost and frightened intrusion wandering around might well find a new home in your next client, your children or in you. If you are doing extractions, make sure that your spirits have given you full instructions about what to do with the intrusion.

CHAPTER FOUR

SOUL RETRIEVAL

Luke came to see me complaining of sinus trouble. He was unable to breathe through his nose, had a constantly running nose and a 'fuzzy head' that would not go away.

I made a shamanic Journey to speak to my healing Teacher in order to ask her what I could do to help Luke. She peered at him.

'He needs a soul retrieval. See.' She pointed at him as he lay on the rug. 'Look at that space.' She studied him closely and then added, 'And there's an intrusion in here. You deal with the intrusion, my dear, while I have a think about this. Breathing … breathing … it's something to do with breathing. The breath of life. He's stopping himself breathing. Breath is life.'

She trailed off and waved me to carry on with the extraction.

I called on more of my spirit helpers and leant over Luke, rattling.

'Get the feather,' said one of my helpers. I reached behind me and picked up the crow feather from my altar. Following instructions, I carried on rattling and waved the feather gently over Luke's face. As I was largely working in Non-ordinary Reality, where I was very aware of the spirits, I could see the small, beetle-like creature look up at me. I sang softly, rattled and waved. The creature crept further out. I sang to it of love and security, assuring it that my spirits would take it home. Slowly it crept up and climbed onto the feather. It was small and shy, only there because Luke's lost soul had left a gap. The intrusion had wandered in and got stuck. I took it over to the open widow and shook the feather out. My power animal, hovering just outside, swooped down, caught the intrusion in his claws and flew off with it, to take it wherever it belonged.

I turned back to Luke and checked that the space was clean and ready for the returning soul. Then I lay down next to him and went fully into Non-ordinary Reality.

I walked to the foot of my tree and began to climb. My Teacher held out her hand and I went over to her.

'Where's your eye?' she asked, mildly.

I stopped in shock. Usually, when I am doing a soul retrieval, my Teacher removes my right eye and replaces it with a spirit eye, which enables me to see the trail that the departing soul leaves. I did not have the eye with me!

'Never mind,' she said, 'let's take out your eye anyway, and put in this pebble instead. Here, wear this eye patch.' She seemed to find the situation amusing.

I wasn't amused. I could hardly see. My spirit helper took my hand and led me off into the out-of-focus mist. Suddenly we were in a grove of trees. In front of us suddenly appeared a figure. At first I couldn't see the figure – largely because of the pebble in my eye socket – but then it coalesced into a large, muscular man, clothed in leaves, breathing life into the stems of foliage that sprang from his mouth. A classic 'Green Man'.

'Are you Luke's soul?' I asked.

He laughed a deep, powerful laugh. Everything about him radiated vigour and energy.

'I am.'

He was taller and broader than Luke was but I could see something of Luke in his eyes.

I explained that I had come looking for him to ask him to return to Luke. He seemed reluctant. I wasn't surprised. He wouldn't have gone in the first place if there were not a good reason. I thought that I had a long argument ahead of me but suddenly he said, 'All right. I'll come back with you if you give me what's behind that eye patch!' Then he stood back, folded his arms and watched me.

Now I knew why my Teacher had been amused. I said, 'Okay.'

Triumphantly he reached out, under the patch, and grabbed the pebble. Then his expression changed. For an instant he looked angry. Then rueful. Then resigned.

'I said I'd come back and I will. But I am Luke's power. I went because he wouldn't believe in me, wouldn't use me. If I come back he won't be able to deny me any more. He'd better be aware of that.'

I agreed. I decided to come back from my Journey to consult with Luke.

I sat up.

'Luke. Your soul is ready to come back if you are ready to accept it but it wants you to know that if it returns you will no longer be able to not use your power.' I paused to let him digest this then added, 'Think about this carefully, Luke. This could completely change your life.'

I left him for a few minutes while I got him a cup of coffee and he thought seriously about what I had told him. When I came back he was determined.

'I came to see you because I wanted things to change. I want you to go ahead and bring the soul back.'

I returned to Non-ordinary Reality and to the Green Man. I told him what Luke had said.

He nodded. 'All right. Let's go.'

He came back with me to Ordinary Reality and I sat up and blew him into Luke's chest.

Because Luke is one of our students, as well as a client and a friend, he has learned to go on a shamanic Journey himself. After a short rest he Journeyed into Non-ordinary Reality to meet his re-united soul. He returned from that Journey with an inner glow and instructions as to how to integrate with the returned soul.

Lynda, Luke's girlfriend, commented when she saw him that evening:

'You're taller!'

People can lose soul for many reasons. Road accidents, for example, are common. In the worst cases it leaves the person unconscious, or in a coma. When someone dies amongst the Pomo Indians of the west coast of America, the deceased is left for three days in case the soul is just wandering and wishes to return. Other traumas lead to soul loss as well. Maybe the most common situation in our society is the giving away of soul. Whenever you do something you feel really bad about, whenever you are in an untenable situation and you give in against your better judgement, you give away power and soul. Very few parents manage to get through parenthood without demanding soul from their children. This isn't to blame parents, necessarily. Children give away soul easily. Martha came to us aware that she was missing something and requested a soul retrieval. She was very surprised when Christine returned with the soul of a six-year-old. A very angry six-year-old. Mum had told her to wear her cardigan. She didn't want to. Trivial, I know, to us as adults but not at all trivial to the six-year-old Martha, who felt that her integrity in being herself had been compromised.

We all find ourselves, occasionally, in situations with dominant people. These may be parents, the boss at work, a spouse or simply a domineering friend. 'He doesn't like it if I … so I don't do that any more.' This kind of self-sacrifice can lead to soul loss. Often the dominant person is not acting in this way in order to be in control. They may genuinely feel that they know what is best for you. And if they are a parent and you are a young child or they are a doctor and you are a patient, for example, they *might* be right. Doing as they say may save your life. In a less dramatic situation it might save your job or your marriage. But the self-sacrifice on your part, whether for good reasons or not, can lead to you giving away power and soul.

One situation where this often happens is at the end of a relationship that you didn't want to end.

'When she left, part of me went with her.'

'I haven't felt complete since the divorce.'

Here, in the UK, we tend not to have soul deliberately stolen as is found in many native societies. Maybe it would happen more often if people knew that soul-stealing was possible. I hope not but most things that are possible are done, regardless of the harm they can cause. What is a lot more common is unintentionally taking soul.

Steven had been ill through all the six years I had known him and for four years before that. Eventually he asked for us for help. When I Journeyed to ask my Teacher she told me that, since the problem concerned Steven's dead girlfriend, Linda, I should let Christine do the work. I can and have worked with the dead, just as Christine heals the living, but these are not our specialities. Christine has a great deal of experience and skill at working with the dead. I returned and told her what my Teacher had said. Then I took over the drumming and Christine went to speak to her Teachers.

I was taken to the outskirts of the Land of the Dead. And there was Linda. She had been dead for ten years but had still not been able to reach the Land of the Dead where she would have been able to receive what healing she needed and where she could have made progress. The reason that she was stuck soon became obvious. In one hand she held Steven. A Steven that was ten years younger but pale and transparent. He hung from her hand.

Linda had died in an accident, a fall from a cliff. Steven had been there at the time. In her shock and terror as she fell she had grabbed at his soul and taken it with her.

Steven couldn't get well without his soul part. Linda couldn't move on while she had it. Christine's job, and that of her spirits, was to persuade Linda to let go of the soul.

You might feel that this would be straightforward – after all, the possession of the soul was doing Linda no good. But when people become stuck after death there is no progression, no moving on. They are stuck in that one moment, spinning around and around. They are caught in the same happening until they get help. This does nothing for their grasp of the situation. Linda was caught in that moment when she fell off the cliff. She still had all the fear that she had had at that moment.

Linda herself needed healing before we could help Steven. Christine and her spirits went to find a power animal that would give Linda the help she needed. Once she had the power that the animal could give her Linda was quite different. The hysteria and the fear had gone. She was able to understand that she was dead and must go on. She gave us a message of love for Steven, handed over his soul and went, with her power animal and the help of Christine's, to the Land of the Dead. Christine brought the soul back to Steven.

Not everyone who takes soul is dead, of course. Sue came to me for healing and I brought back two pieces of soul. One had gone when she was a baby and, in the first days of her life, she had been without her mother who was seriously ill. The other had gone at the age of eight when Sue had got lost in a park and had been very frightened. These were straightforward and were quickly brought back. But Sue had a part of someone else's soul. She had recently split up with Peter after twelve years of living together. She had a piece of Peter's soul. Like Linda, Sue was unable to progress along her life's path hampered by soul that wasn't hers. Unlike Linda, Sue was still alive and anxious to be well. She was also concerned that Peter couldn't start this new phase of his life without her if he was without some of his soul.

I asked my Teachers how best to deal with this and, acting on their advice, took the piece of Peter's soul and put it into an envelope. Sue went home, visited Peter and told him what had happened. She then gave him the envelope. Two weeks later, Peter visited me himself, amazed at how much happier and lighter he felt.

Peter was interested in spiritual matters and was very open to the work that Sue told him about. It isn't always so, of course. Your boss or your mother may well not want to have anything to do with a returning soul piece. When this has happened I have given the soul to my spirit Teacher and she has taken it somewhere where it will be safe. I would not do healing for anyone without his or her permission.

Helen was not well. She thought it might be stress, particularly since her mother, Sandra, who had had psychiatric problems for several years, had just had a stroke. She was depressed and exhausted.

My Teacher took me to see Helen. She instructed me to rattle and, as I did so, observed Helen closely. Suddenly she pointed. 'Look, my dear. There's soul missing here. See?' She carefully removed my eye and replaced it with the spirit eye.

Instantly I could see a bright blue thread stretching away into the distance. This was the path that the departing soul piece had taken. With my Teacher, I set off. At the other end of the thread we found Sandra. She sat in a darkened room with a tangle of knitting wool and needles in her lap. The blue thread disappeared into her knitting basket.

'Go away!' she shouted at me.

'I've come to see if I can help you,' I said.

'Well you can't,' she snapped. 'I told you to go away.'

I wasn't at all sure what to do but my Teacher reached into the basket and pulled out not only a part of Helen but also parts of Sandra's husband, her other children, her parents and many souls that I did not recognise. Sandra leapt up.

'They're mine! Leave them alone!' She swung at us with her stick. We ducked the swing and my Teacher, after handing me Helen's soul, took the rest to the window and flung them out. They scattered like brightly coloured birds.

I said to my Teacher, 'Is there anything I can do for Sandra?'

She replied, 'Has she asked you to do anything?'

She hadn't. We left and I brought Helen's soul back to her.

I don't know where the other souls went. At least they were no longer in captivity. Helen was much better. Her depression lifted and she had a far more cheerful outlook on life.

Sandra, prevented by her mental problems from adopting the positive outlook that is so helpful to stroke victims, continued to get weaker. She took out her frustrations on her family and on the nursing-home staff. Helen, although feeling much better in herself and able to cope, was, of course, distressed by her mother's state. Then Sandra's daughter-in-law, Tina, confided to me that, although not dead, Sandra was haunting her.

I have read of cases where a living person has visited somewhere in a dream and has been seen by the waking people in that place as a ghost. Could something similar be happening with Sandra? I asked my Teacher. And was told yes, of course. Sandra, who was in a dream-like state for much of the time anyway, was flinging off parts of her soul in order to harm those against whom she had a grudge. And because of her mental problems there were many of those. For years she had taken as little responsibility as was possible for the things that had happened to her. Everything was 'someone else's fault'.

In her vehemence she was visiting Tina, standing at the foot of her bed and hurling anger and fear at her. Tina had begun by simply knowing that she would wake sometimes in the night, terrified of something at the end of the bed. But Tina was more sensitive than she herself realised. As Sandra's fury became more directed and she projected more and more of herself towards Tina she became more recognisable.

'I know it's Sandra,' said Tina, who was, naturally, very upset.

I asked my Teacher for help with the problem and was told that I, with my Teacher's help, should approach Sandra.

Sandra lay on her hospital bed. She was consumed with anger and was projecting towards me the image of her with long, sharp teeth and claws. Ferocious though this figure was she was also nearly transparent.

My Teacher said, 'See, she has thrown off so much of herself that there's very little left.'

I asked what we should do and my Teacher told me to watch.

Then she unwrapped what at first appeared to be a bundle of cloth but turned out to be a golden net. She spread it over the nursing home.

'Now she can't send any more of herself out.'

'And the parts that have already gone?' I asked.

'Don't worry,' she said, 'I'll deal with those.'

I was still concerned about Sandra's transparency. She had obviously lost a great deal of soul. Was there any way I could bring it back to her? My Teacher shook her head.

'She doesn't want it back, you know. She's spent a very long time not wanting to be well so that others could take care of her. This is a result of that.'

I felt terribly sorry for Sandra but I could see what my Teacher meant. I had known the family for several years and Sandra had, all that time, courted ill health in order to have others look after her and give them their attention. I knew that, in some ways, this was both the cause and the result of her mental problems; an ever-tightening spiral of suspicion and distrust.

My Teacher gathered together the soul parts that Sandra had thrown off and took them away. When I asked where they had gone I was told that they were in a place that was neither the Land of the Dead nor was it in this material realm. It was a place where she could rest, in a location she had constructed for herself. This can happen when someone is between life and death, belonging neither here nor in the Land of the Dead. Sandra had built herself a garden where she could surround herself with the flowers that she had loved when she had been well.

When she died, two years later, her parts were able to be reunited and she was taken, whole again, to the Land of the Dead where she can get the healing that she needs.

When I first did this work with Sandra I had not come across the idea of parts of the soul 'being kept safe' rather than being returned to the owner. Since then it has cropped up once or twice more, and always in situations where bringing the soul back might do more harm than good.

May, for example, a woman in her eightiess, has had four strokes. Her body is unable to do much more than lie in bed all day. What good would be done by bringing back the major part of her soul to her hospital bed? Better to leave it where it is, happily in a garden. May, like Sandra, had loved flowers.

Thankfully, I don't have to make decisions about such things. Shamanism allows me to speak with May's soul and to know that she is happy to wait in her garden until her body dies and she can go to the Land of the Dead. And my Teacher is always an ethical guide in such matters.

During the first workshop that Christine and I ran, several years ago, I became worried about one of our students. Mick seemed to me to be very ungrounded. He spoke about drifting out of his body without intention and 'hovering about the ceiling'. When the students Journeyed, Mick was able easily to move 'out of body' but not to enter the spirit realms. He was stuck within a few feet of his physical body.

I pointed out that his experience, while undoubtedly 'out of body', was not shamanic Journeying. He was unable to contact any helper spirits. Mick, however, was quite happy with what he was used to.

After the workshop I asked my spirits what the problem was and they introduced me to a boy of about twelve.

'This is Mick,' my Teacher said. 'He's been wandering around for nearly twenty years now. Because the rest of Mick's soul knows that something is missing it keeps trying to leave his body to search for the missing bit. But Mick's spirit helpers, even though he has not yet met them, won't let him go far. He has so little soul left that if more went he might not survive.'

I looked at the boy.

'What should I do with him?' I asked. 'Mick hasn't asked me for a soul retrieval.'

'We'll keep him safe,' my Teacher said. 'You tell Mick about it.'

It was a strange thing to do to write a letter to someone I hardly knew, telling him that my spirits were looking after part of his soul. Mick did come for a soul retrieval and when he did the work was straightforward. After all, I knew exactly where to go to fetch the soul. But it took seventeen months between the letter being sent and Mick feeling that he was ready to be whole.

A soul retrieval is deep work and, like any such work, brings change. And change cannot be forced upon someone else – at least, not by another person. The spirits can give the occasional shove. Even then, it's more a case of letting us know that it's time to move rather than the move itself. We have to take responsibility for ourselves. Otherwise, what will we have learned? Sandra Ingerman, in her book *Soul Retrieval – Mending the Fragmented Self*, mentions a case where a young woman realised that she was not ready to cope with health. That young woman's choice not to have back a piece of soul has to be respected. I admire the fact that she knew what she could deal with. More common is a situation where someone thinks that they want to be well without really understanding the consequences of not being able to fall back into the comfort zone of illness.

Tom came to me for help. He felt that he had no real direction in life and no enthusiasm for anything. I asked my Teachers what to do and was told to check that Tom really did want his life to change. Tom said he did. So I went.

My spirits took me, for a long time, through skies of stars and planets. Eventually we came upon a cave, floating in space, a hollow rock. We stepped inside and found a wooden, brass-bound chest. Inside was a small boy of about seven, dressed in a grey and red school uniform. As I raised the lid he huddled down further into a corner of the chest. I tried to coax him out, to no avail, and finally left the talking to my spirits, who can be much more gentle and persuading than I.

Soon the boy had emerged and was sitting on my Teacher's knee. He confirmed that he was Tom and said that he had left because he couldn't be himself because of his very possessive mother. He would come back only if Tom would distance himself from his mother. He also said that 'the other one' had to come back as well.

'What other one?' I asked. The seven-year-old Tom took us to a place where an island rose out of a blue sea. The sort of island that a soul who had read and enjoyed Swiss Family Robinson *or* The Coral Island *might have made for itself. There was a fresh-water stream and fruit on the trees. There was a small wooden hut with fish cooking over a fire in front of it.*

From out of the trees came a young man in his early twenties. He was good-looking and much slimmer than the Tom that I knew. He had also much more vitality than the present-day Tom.

He echoed what his younger self had said, that he would not return unless Tom were prepared to disengage himself from his mother. After all, Tom was now in his late thirties, living by himself some forty miles from his mother. I came back to Ordinary Reality and told Tom what the souls had said.

He was agreeable and I went back to tell them that all was sorted and they returned with me. I blew them into Tom.

I had underestimated Tom's reluctance to change. Oh, yes, he wanted to be rid of his depression and his sinus troubles and his high blood pressure. But he didn't want to make the major life-changes that were required. In particular he did not want to examine his relationship with his mother. Sometime later my Teacher took me on a Journey.

My Teacher took me to a place where an island rose out of a blue sea. The sort of island that a soul who had read and enjoyed Swiss Family Robinson *or* The Coral Island *might have made for itself. There was a fresh-water stream and fruit on the trees. There was a small wooden hut with fish cooking over a fire in front of it.*

From out of the trees came a young man in his early twenties. He waved when he saw me. I went up to him.

'I'm sorry,' I said, 'I shouldn't have taken you back. Tom wasn't ready.'

'No,' he agreed, 'but it was an interesting experience. If Tom does become ready for us and asks for your help when he is seriously ready to take responsibility for himself, we'll come back.'

'We?' I asked.

He grinned. From out of the hut came the seven-year-old.

'We're staying together until we can go back to Tom.'

They seemed perfectly happy and I left them there.

That was an important teaching for me. There is no point in bringing back a soul part unless the situation that caused it to leave has been rectified.

Pauline asked me to do some work, both for herself and for her boyfriend, Martin, who was in prison. I brought Pauline a soul part that had gone missing but my Teacher said that it was inappropriate to do the same for Martin. It was being in prison that had caused his soul loss. Bringing back the part that had gone, the part that could not cope with being imprisoned, could only make things worse for both the soul part and for Martin.

I don't want to make it sound, when talking about taking responsibility for our own health, that I consider people to blame for their own illnesses or conditions. I don't. Nothing in my experience or what I have learned from others' experiences leads me to think that.

Of course, we contribute to our own conditions. Sandra contributed to her stroke because she wanted to be ill so that others would be put into the position of having to look after her. But to suggest that she was fully responsible for her own illness is to ignore all the factors that contributed to her attitude from her childhood, her adulthood and her past lives.

But the fact is that no one else can take responsibility for your health. Not once you are an independent adult, at any rate. Only you can decide to change your life, whether this means giving up smoking, moving away from a polluted area or investigating the spiritual aspects of your illnesses. Not because they are your fault but because no one else can do it for you. To take blame is to feel that you have done something to make the situation worse. To take responsibility is to feel that you are able to make the situation better.

Having a soul retrieval changes your life. There is no way that having part of yourself brought back couldn't change your life. But sometimes it does it in very unexpected ways. Think of Tom and the mental and physical problems that led him to visit me in the first place. He was not expecting these problems to have their spiritual cause in the fact that he was unwilling and unable to move further away from the sphere of his mother's possessiveness.

Belinda came to see us because she was 'stuck'. She was worn out with caring for three children by herself and seemed, in her own words, 'to be giving out all the time'. Although it might seem completely normal to be tired under such circumstances, Belinda was depressed by her feeling of being trapped. I brought her back a piece of soul that had left with her husband. Souls often come back with conditions. After all, no soul wants to return to a situation the same or worse than it left. Belinda's soul told me, and I told Belinda, that it would come back to stay if, and only if, she made some big changes. One of these was that she and her children should move house, away from the place that would always be associated with the life they had had before Belinda's husband moved out. Belinda went home and put the house on the market. The effects of soul retrieval can be instantaneous but usually take some days or even weeks to filter through. In this case Belinda telephoned me about ten days later to say:

'I've realised I'm free. I've just put these chains on myself. I need to cut them. Now I feel that I can.'

Mary came to see us because of stress. She was very angry and tense, screaming at other road users. She assumed that anyone who pulled out into the road in front of her had deliberately 'cut her up'. She had stand-up rows with other drivers because they had 'stolen' her parking space. Classic examples of road rage.

Christine did the soul retrieval for Mary. The spiritual cause of her anger lay back in her childhood when, at the age of four, distressed by her parents' continual rows, the part of her that could least cope with the situation had left. Since the part that could least cope with conflict had gone the part that was left found it easy to give way to fury. But anger in itself throws off parts of our souls. Just as Sandra had done, Mary was firing off tiny bits of soul every time she lost her temper. People who say, 'I was beside myself with anger' might well be speaking the literal truth. Not that every flash of anger causes soul loss, but when a key part, such as Mary's four-year-old, has gone others follow more easily. Christine described these others as 'onion skins', collected them up and brought them back to Mary.

Two days later Mary was driving along a main road when someone came up behind her, close and fast. Mary pulled over into a lay-by and let the driver overtake and get well away. Then she continued her journey safely. She was so amazed that she telephoned us to tell us all about it.

I learned about the effects that a soul retrieval can have one December several years ago when I had an eight-year-old part returned to me. At the time I was thirty-nine and had been studying shamanism for about three years. The immediate effect was tiredness. I sought out my teddy bear, who for about thirty years had lived on various bookshelves, and went to bed for a week. When I got up again Teddy went back on the shelf and I indulged a sudden craving for chocolate and lemon ice-cream, a taste I'd developed in Italy the summer I was seven. The tiredness and the desire for ice-cream went but there were some totally unlooked-for effects that have lasted.

My father, when younger, was a renowned climber and, on summer evenings and weekends, we would go out of Sheffield to the Derbyshire gritstone edges. Round about the time I was eight I began to worry about falling. I carried on climbing for most of my teenage years, but never with the confidence I had had before. As I started to go out more by myself I moved away from climbing to mountain walking in the Lake District and Scotland. By my late thirties I couldn't stand on balconies or cross suspension bridges. Then, in the January following my soul retrieval, a friend asked us to go caving. And I discovered that I loved it. On our third trip he brought a thirty-foot ladder and, after securing one end, dropped the other into the darkness of a hole.

'Who's going first?' he asked, cheerfully.

'She is,' said Christine, pointing at me. So I took a deep breath and stepped forward onto the ladder, waiting for the fear to hit me. And it didn't. I climbed down the ladder, the darkness lit only by my helmet-lamp, discovered that the ladder ended about five feet above the cave floor and jumped. I was having the time of my life! It had never occurred to me that regaining a piece of soul could result in me losing my fear of heights.

I told my sister about it the following summer when we visited her in Hong Kong. I wasn't sure if she believed me. After all, I'd had a fear of heights for all of her life. On the last night of our stay she and her husband took us for a drink. We got into the lift at the Hopewell Centre and started to go up. And suddenly Hong Kong was spread below us! The lift to the revolving restaurant on the seventy-second floor is, from the seventeenth to the seventy-first floor, on the outside of the building. As it is made of glass the view is stupendous. My sister was left in no doubt at all.

I know that there are people who do soul retrievals by telephone or even over the Internet. Be careful of this type of arrangement. I'm sure that in some cases it can work well, although it is difficult to assess the degree of connection between a practitioner and his or her spirits unless you can meet and talk with that practitioner. I have done distance work but only in emergency and only when I know the client beforehand. Suppose something comes up during the work that you find emotionally hard. Do you really want the person who is helping you to be miles away on the other end of a telephone line? What if there are problems? Will you, inexperienced as you may be, recognise them? Will your practitioner recognise them from a distance? With the returning soul can come memories and emotions that you have not experienced since the part went. Is this something you want to happen when your practitioner is not there to help you? And where, in distance healing, is the connection, the sense of community? Can distance healing sometimes be simply an excuse not to engage with others?

Be as careful when choosing a shamanic practitioner as you would be when choosing anyone else who is to do intimate and life-changing work with you. At the end of this book are the addresses and telephone numbers of reputable organisations that can put you in contact with trained and experienced shamanic practitioners. When you first contact a practitioner don't be afraid to ask questions. Any practitioner who won't answer questions about his or her experience, training or methods probably isn't someone that you should be trusting with your soul.

If you decide to have a soul retrieval you will probably feel better for having some idea about what is likely to happen. Soul retrievals are, usually, less noisy than extractions. Having said that, there will still be rattling and drumming.

Most practitioners will start off by talking to you and listening to you. Talking to you about shamanism and listening to what you have to say about your problem. He or she will usually be happy to hear whatever you wish to tell them. This helps the practitioner have an overview of the problem but intimate details will probably not be necessary – unless it helps you to talk about them, of course. The spirits are the ones who direct the work and they will know what is needed.

When the drumming starts the practitioner will probably lie down beside you, touching you in some way. I find that holding hands is both comforting and not too intrusive. Some shamans (for example, the Tuvans) stand up and dance and drum themselves into a trance Journey. However, lying down is the most common way for a modern shamanic practitioner to Journey. During this time you need do nothing other than relax and listen to the drumming. The practitioner is Journeying, with his or her spirit helpers, to find your lost soul. Then the practitioner will sit up. I use a crystal to carry the soul part back to Ordinary Reality, so I would place the crystal against – unless the spirits have told me otherwise – your solar plexus and then I would blow the soul out of the crystal, into you. Then I would ask you to sit up and blow any residue of soul into the top of your head. I have, very occasionally, had to blow the soul into other parts of the body. That is up to my spirits. I *always* consult the client before I do anything that involves touching them. Other practitioners may use other items as a soul carrier – I know one woman who uses her wristwatch. Or the practitioner may use his or her hands.

I mentioned that an extraction badly done can harm the practitioner. A soul retrieval badly done can harm the client.

Barbara came to me very upset. She knew a little about shamanism having done a two-day introductory workshop. Three weeks prior to her visiting me she had been on another workshop, one where the teacher had taught shamanic healing. And on this workshop she had had a soul retrieval. She told me that the student who had done the retrieval had brought her back a part she had lost as a baby. The baby was distressed and ill. He had blown it into her as instructed.

Barbara did daily meditation. She found that every time she settled to meditate she could hear the baby crying. Then she could hear it whenever she tried to relax. Then while she was doing routine jobs. After a couple of weeks she could hear it constantly. She could not sleep and she felt sick and scared.

In itself it was a simple case. With my Teacher's help I extracted the baby, my Teacher healed it and I blew it back into Barbara. But what an experience. And one that could so easily have been avoided if the student doing the work had known enough to take the baby to his Teacher to be healed before he had brought it back in the first place. And also, since it was on a workshop and therefore ultimately the responsibility of the workshop teacher, if that teacher had mentioned the possibility of a soul in need of healing.

Your practitioner should tell you a few things afterwards. What you should do to prevent the soul part from going again, for example, or under what conditions it has agreed to come back at all. These are things that usually I ask the soul before I bring it back. If, as in the case of Luke, the soul wants something that I do not feel able to promise on the client's behalf I will consult with the client before going back to talk to the soul. Another thing your practitioner should pass on to you from the spirits is how the soul should be integrated. Some practitioners do not mention integration. Reputable ones do. After all, you don't want to be an adult with a separate five-year-old inside you for the rest of your life, do you? You want to be one complete being. Only if my client studies shamanism and can go and ask the soul directly do I leave the question of integration. If you, the client, can Journey it is a wonderful ending to a soul retrieval session for you to visit your own soul and talk to it.

And then there are the after-effects, which I have already written about. Expect to be tired. A soul retrieval is the spiritual equivalent of major surgery. Don't be surprised, particularly if the soul that has returned went as a child, by a desire, as I had, for ice-cream or, as happened to a friend, an urge to play on a swing. If these things happen, give in to them. They won't last (unless they are a part of you that you have needed, such as the ability to laugh) and they won't do any harm. Pamper yourself for a while. You have just had a very important part of yourself returned.

A rather more disturbing side-effect is, as I said before, the possible return of the thoughts and feelings that you had at the time the soul left. This can be traumatic simply because it was trauma of some kind that led to the part going in the first place. If this happens please bear in mind that they are only the *memories* of the thoughts and feelings. The reality that caused them is long gone and the damage done by them, the loss of soul, has just been mended. If it is very bad get back to your practitioner, as you should do if you experience any problems, but usually these memories pass gently away, leaving you a stronger and more powerful person.

So where do the soul parts go? Well, the soul, when separated from its body, either during soul loss or at death, often stays, confused and locked in the moment of trauma, exactly where the original incident took place. When Julie, who was a teacher in an inner-city comprehensive, learned that one of her pupils was in hospital, having had petrol poured over him and been set alight by his friends, she was shocked. Months after the boy was out of hospital and back in school, she was still traumatised by the event, unable to put the experience behind her and move on. I found her soul still sitting in the staff room, still huddled in the corner, still caught in that moment when she first heard the news.

Some souls flee back to where they have felt safe in the past. When Lucy was leaving her beloved childhood home in the Far East, nearly forty years ago, she was indecently assaulted by a steward on the ship. The soul that left then took quite some tracking down. Eventually it was found outside a school in the road where Lucy had once lived. It had run back to the family's old flat and had stayed there for many years, until the block of flats had been demolished. Then it had wandered, forlorn, along the street until, attracted by the children's voices near the school, it had taken up residence amongst the trees across the road.

Many souls wander off and get lost – one I retrieved was living in a derelict row of terraced houses – and many, particularly if they are escaping someone in particular, hide.

If you have read Sandra Ingerman's *Soul Retrieval* you will have read about 'the Cave of Lost Children'. This appears to be a particularly grey and cheerless place where children's souls are either taken, or take refuge. I believe this to be the same place that I think of as 'the Orphanage', a forbidding Victorian edifice with tall, spiked railings around it. Maybe 'archetype' is the right word here. I'm not sure. My 'gut feeling' about it is that we see the place as we expect to see a place where children are, possibly kept against their wills, certainly without play or laughter. Who runs it? Who rounds up the souls of lost children to incarcerate them? I'm still trying to find out these answers. When I tracked down Andy's soul part that was where he was – in the yard outside the grey orphanage. The sort of place that began life as a workhouse, then became an orphanage. Now, in the twenty-first century, in our reality, most have thankfully gone, demolished to make way for sunnier, happier places. A few linger on as mental hospitals or old people's homes – putting those most in need of sunshine into the shadows. In Non-ordinary Reality this was what met my eyes:

> *No sun, no real colour in the place, children in grey clothes, with grey faces, milling aimlessly. I asked my spirit helper where Andy was and he pointed. Andy looked to be about ten and had a*

pinched, miserable face. I tried to persuade him to come with us but, to begin with, he seemed scared, looking around him as if someone were about to come and stop us. Then he looked resigned.

'There's no point,' he said. 'No one wants me.'

Is that a clue, I wonder? Is it the children who feel unloved and unwanted who end up here? And is the place as much manufactured by their expectations as by mine? My spirit helper stepped in and persuaded him eventually that it was worth the risk of coming with us. Suddenly the other children became aware of me and hundreds of tiny hands on thin, bony arms reached out to grab me. My spirit helper gripped me in one hand and Andy in the other and leapt to safety.

When I got back from this Journey I felt strange, floaty, unable to concentrate. My Teacher took one look at me and sent me back with my spirit helper. We returned to the orphanage and my spirit helper left me outside the railings while he went inside to rescue the part of me that the desperate children had grabbed.

A similar 'archetypal' (no, I'm not happy with that word. I can't think of a better!) place is 'the City'. Tracy had lost a soul part when she had been in a relationship with a domineering boyfriend. I and my spirits tracked it down to a huge city.

I thought at first that it was Newcastle, since the first thing I recognised was the Tyne Bridge. Then I saw that, beyond the bridge, there was the Eiffel Tower! I looked around more carefully and spotted the Lincoln Memorial.

'What is this place?' I asked my spirit helper.

'It's the City,' he said.

'What city?'

'The City that is the idea behind all cities. Many lost souls find their way here. Cities suck people in.'

We walked streets that could have been in any city. Eventually my spirit helper indicated a huddled figure in a doorway. The figure was wrapped in a faded blanket and had an old, cloth cap at its feet, for collecting coins. We stood in front of it. At last it raised its head and revealed itself to be a slightly younger Tracy. I greeted her. She was brusque and suspicious. Gradually I got her to talk to me. She was the

*part of Tracy that was fiercely independent – that would rather live
homeless on the streets of the City than be subjugated (as she saw it) to
her boyfriend. She was not mollified by the news that Tracy had left that
boyfriend and was now living with another young man, in a much
more equal relationship. Quite frankly, she didn't believe it! Finally I
persuaded her to return with me on the condition that Tracy had three
weeks in which to prove that things had changed. If the soul was not
convinced by that time she would leave again.*

Although some cultures believe, and some shamanic teachers teach,
that all souls, when they are lost, go to the Land of the Dead, this
has not been my experience. Perhaps, in other cultures, the way to
the Land of the Dead is more defined, more known by the general
populace, than it is here. I have rescued very few souls from the Land
of the Dead. There seem to be three main reasons that lost souls find
their ways to the Land of the Dead. One is that some soul part stayed
there when the main soul left to be born. This is usually because the
soul was in two minds about being born. Or it might be that some
accident or illness at birth, or problem (for example neglect) just
after birth causes part of the baby to return while it is still aware of
the way. I did a soul retrieval recently for a woman whose mother had
developed a severe illness immediately after my client's birth and had
been unable to take care of her baby. Part of the infant's soul had
gone back to the Land of the Dead, feeling unloved and unwanted.
Although, intellectually, my client understood that her mother had
not harmed her deliberately and, indeed, could not consciously
remember being deprived of her mother at that crucial stage of her
life, there had always been an awkwardness between the two of them.

The third reason for a soul part returning to the Land of the
Dead usually happens later in life. If an accident or illness occurs that
is severe enough to convince the soul that it is dying, it may well set
off by itself to the Land of the Dead, supposing that the rest of the
soul parts are close behind it. I know about this from my own experience. When I was a child I contracted viral pneumonia. Everyone,
including my soul, expected me to die. But I didn't. Many years later
I had a soul retrieval that was brought back from the Land of the
Dead. Afterwards, I Journeyed to ask the soul part why it had gone.

'I was very ill,' it said to me, 'and I was dying. So I set off to go to the Land of the Dead. I thought all of me was together. But when I got there, I couldn't get in because I wasn't a complete soul. So I waited here, at the edge of the Land of the Dead, until the rest of me caught up. But instead, someone came and brought me back to you.'

Many soul parts have some awareness that the 'primary part' is still continuing in the situation from which they have escaped. This part of mine had a different perspective. As far as she was concerned, she was the primary piece and I had been 'retrieved' for her!

The last place that souls sometimes go that I want to tell you about is called, by my Teachers, 'the Void'. This is a huge, dark and deep chasm, somewhere near the Land of the Dead. It appears to be a 'holding place' of some sort, for those souls so damaged that they are unable to enter the Land of the Dead, even to those parts concerned with healing. I don't know what goes on in the Void. Those souls that I have seen being sent there have been very disturbed. One was a psychopathic murderer, and this seems, from what my Teachers tell me, to be typical. This is not a place of punishment, although it cannot be pleasant, but rather somewhere that something very slow and deep and, eventually, healing takes place. I do know that, after a very long time, the soul can come out, ready to continue on its path. 'Nothing is forever,' my Teacher tells me.

But, at the moment, we are interested in the Void not as a place of the dead but as a place where lost souls might wander in and be unable to find their ways out. And this does happen. Sometimes because the soul part, when it leaves, is so panic-stricken that it falls in accidentally, and sometimes because the soul part it too preoccupied with something else.

Nancy was obsessed with a particular man who had died several years before. Although there had been no relationship between them while he had been alive (indeed, they had never met. She had seen him only on television), Nancy had been distraught at his death. Now she wanted to be well, and rid of her obsession. Christine did the soul retrieval and these are her notes.

'We are only just in time,' said my Teacher. He took me to a Place where we found Nancy and **** (the man – Christine recognised him, he had been moderately famous in his day). They were joined together by a thick pipe inside which something flowed. Behind them was a deep pit of nothing. My Teacher said, 'They are on the edge of the Void. We must be careful. If we move quickly or suddenly they could tip into the Void and be lost.'

I asked him what to do. He considered and then told me to go to Nancy and distract her – 'Point out those flowers to her' – and then, on his word, hold her shoulders firmly and pull.

'Hello, Nancy,' I said. 'Have you seen these pretty flowers?'

She turned her head.

'Now!' commanded my Teacher. I took hold of her shoulders and pulled her. My Teacher severed the pipe. It snaked back to **** and melted. The stuff inside the pipe rushed to Nancy, red and healthy-looking. It covered her and was absorbed by her, leaving her looking bright and sparkly. I brought her back.

This work not only allowed Nancy to continue her life unhampered by having part of her soul missing, but also allowed **** to be taken, by Christine and her spirits, to the Land of the Dead, where he could have the healing that he needed.

I have done several soul retrievals from the Void. My spirit helpers always fly in with me and I do not touch the sides. There seems to be no light except for a glow given off by my spirit helpers and by some of the souls there. I have never reached the bottom, although once I went so deep, searching for someone, that I could hear rushing water somewhere far below me. The souls huddle on ledges and seem to be unaware of each other.

I said, in the chapter on Healing, that the shamanic practitioner does not heal him- or herself. This is particularly true of soul retrievals, for all the reasons that I mentioned in chapter three and one other very good one. It was you that the soul part left. This sounds harsh and I do not mean it to sound as if you are an unpleasant person to be with, but the soul part went because, in a particular situation, it wanted to behave in a different way from the rest of you.

Almost every healing requires you to change. For some people this change may be drastic. If, for example, your soul loss has left you feeling so empty and careless of yourself that you are drinking heavily to dull the pain, then the soul part may well refuse to come back until you promise that you will stop drinking. Because you probably need the soul part in order to be able to stop drinking, the shamanic practitioner will negotiate between you. Maybe the solution will be that the soul part returns for a month. In that month you will have at least to reduce your alcohol intake.

Many changes will not seem so enormous, at least, not until you have seen the changes in your life for yourself. Maybe your soul part wants you to stick up for yourself more, or to like yourself better. These may seem very easy to say 'yes' to until we start to examine carefully how we could 'work on' these issues. Having a shamanic practitioner who can negotiate with your soul part is very valuable.

When you are in a relationship, whether that is between lovers, a parent and child, siblings or any other connection, there is a constant flow of energy between you. Please don't think that this is the same as power or soul loss. This energy flow is both natural and good. But, occasionally, we do get into situations where soul or power is lost. A row, maybe, or just the irritations of life together where he is always just where you need to be in the kitchen and why can't she ever fold the newspaper after she's read it? You know the kind of thing I mean. What I'm going to suggest now is not a substitute for a soul retrieval. It will not heal major soul loss. But it might make life just that little bit more smooth. My Teacher gave me this little exercise, several years ago. It has served Christine and me well. My Teacher now wants me to share it with you, in the hope that you also will benefit from it.

First get the agreement of your partner. It's not a good basis for any relationship to sneak healing in behind his or her back. Then pour yourselves each a glass of water, or wine, or cola. Whatever drink you both like. With intention, for it is the intention, in life as in Journeying, that forms the boundaries of what will happen, say, 'I put into this glass any parts of you that I should not have.'

Exchange drinks with your partner. Drink, being aware that anything you have been missing has been returned to you and that anything you had of your partner's has now gone back to where it should be.

CHAPTER FIVE

•••••••••••••••••••••••••••••

THE LAND OF THE DEAD

My grandmother was a bitter woman who had lived a hard life. She had been widowed long before I was born and my father was the oldest of four children. When she died, several years ago, there was a sense of relief in the rest of the family. She had had far too little happiness to be able to spread any around to the rest of us.

About three years after she died I learned to Journey to the Land of the Dead. My spirits were very careful with me, giving me rules by which to conduct myself while I was there. I was not to let go of my spirit Teacher and I was not to touch anything, including the ground. Luckily, as long as I held on to my Teacher I was able to float about six inches above the ground. My Teacher told me there was someone for me to meet.

> *In front of me was a lawn, sloping gently towards a clear stream before rising again beyond it. On the far bank of the stream stood two figures, wrapped in each other's arms. I approached slowly, reluctant to disturb them, but then I realised that there was nothing I could do that was at all likely to disturb them in any way. They were totally engrossed in each other. I recognised one from photographs of my grandfather. The other, I realised, was my grandmother, younger and certainly happier than I had ever seen her. I came away and left them to their embrace.*

A couple of years later I went back.

> *I went to the same place but there was no one there. Then, as I floated by the stream wondering where to go, my grandparents*

71

*walked towards me, hand in hand. My grandmother was smiling –
something that she did, in life, rarely.*

*'Jane, I'd like you to meet someone.' She drew her husband closer
and said to me, 'This is your grandfather.'*

*They were clearly as very much in love as they had been when alive.
My Teacher would not allow me to touch them but I could feel the
happiness and love radiating from them.*

There is always a great deal of curiosity about the Land of the Dead.
Of course we want to know what it's like. After all, we're all going
to go there eventually, aren't we? There are a few ways that we can
find out at least some of the details. Although shamanic practitioners don't visit the Land of the Dead as a matter of course, at least
not in our culture, we do occasionally have to go there.

Her spirits had told Catherine that she needed a soul retrieval.
This did not come as a surprise to either Catherine or myself.
Catherine had been doing a lot of work on her problems. Her
parents had separated when she was four and her father had died
when Catherine was fifteen. Catherine had also been told by her
spirits that her father had something else of hers. We prepared for
the Journey.

I set out to see Catherine's father.

*My spirits led me to the outskirts of the Land of the Dead. Here
a grey fog swirls and there is little to see, but I knew, from past
experience, that we were very close to the edge of the Void. Dimly,
through the fog, I could see the thin blue line of light that leads to a
missing soul part. I followed it and found a man standing in the fog,
holding tightly onto a toddler and a teenager. My spirit helper handed
me a black box, so large that I had to hold it in both arms.*

*'When we get them, don't touch them! We'll put them straight into
here,' he said. I opened the box in readiness and we closed in on the
man, who, I realised, was Catherine's father. When he saw me he
clutched the two souls of his daughter close to him.*

'You can't take them. They're mine!' he shouted.

While he was so agitated my spirit helper darted in and grabbed hold of the teenager. She was limp between the two of them. Suddenly there was a tug and my spirit helper had her. He pushed her into the box and I closed the lid.

Her father was furious. He took the toddler and held her over his head.

'Come any closer,' he yelled, 'and I'll throw her in there!' He took a few steps towards the Void.

At that moment two figures approached from the direction of the Land of the Dead. They were dressed in white coats and they introduced themselves as 'orderlies'. They moved nearer to Catherine's father and he swung his daughter into the air and threw her over the edge of the Void.

The orderlies took hold of Catherine's father's arms. They began to walk with him back the way they had come. Then they paused and turned to me.

'Take that one back first, then come and seek the little one. We will look after him.' They led him away.

I hurried back to my Teacher with the box full of Catherine's teenage soul. When I got there my Teacher took it out of my hands.

'I'll deal with this,' she said. 'You go and fetch the other.'

I went back to the Void where my spirit helper stood and looked down.

The Void is deep and dark. I looked at my helper. He is very big and strong. He produced a rope from somewhere and tied it around my waist. He gave me a net. Then I leapt in.

I began to drift downwards, slowly. Nothing seems to happen quickly in the Void but this was slower than usual. I twisted myself around and dived head first in an attempt to gain a little speed. This seemed to work. There are few points of reference in the Void but, far below me, I could see the little girl falling still and, as far as I could tell, I was gaining on her. I concentrated on going still faster.

There she was! I swooped below her and caught her in the net. At once, my spirit helper began to pull me up.

Eventually I stood once again on the edge of the Void, with my helper. He put the little girl into the box so that I didn't need to touch her, then we returned to my Teacher. She placed the box on the table in her house and helped the two girls out of their boxes. They sat on the edge of the table and we all looked at each other.

The teenager was quiet and unhappy, but was prepared to talk to us about returning to Catherine. The toddler was furious.

'I want my daddy! I hate you! I love my daddy!'

My Teacher said, 'Leave her with me. You have to speak to the Guardians.'

Once more I set off for the Land of the Dead.

This time I went to the main entrance and stood outside the gates. I called out, 'I need to speak to the Guardians.'

After what seemed a long time the gates opened, silently. Three figures came out. They were extremely tall and very thin. They were dressed in grey robes that hid all of them, including their hands and faces, and when they moved they glided across the ground.

'Who are you?' They spoke in unison.

I introduced myself, giving my spirit name, the one my spirits gave me when I began to take shamanism seriously, and explained that I was a shaman with a client who needed to speak with her father. I told them that her father had something of hers that she needed back.

For a while they stood soundlessly, although I had the feeling that they were communicating with each other. Then they said, 'Bring her to the Cottage.'

They turned and glided back into the Land of the Dead. Silently, the gates closed behind them. I went back to my Teacher's house.

Eventually we persuaded both soul parts that they should come back to Catherine. But Catherine still had the task of going to see her father and asking him for that which he had of hers – her confidence. I began drumming and she set off on her Journey. This is her account of that Journey.

I found myself in fog, all around me. The only thing to see was a small cottage with a lawned garden in front of it surrounded by a picket fence. A straight path ran from the door to the gate in the fence. Around the garden was about four feet of solid ground before the fog began. My father was coming down the path towards me. He said, 'Hello.' I said to him, 'I think you have something of mine.' He agreed that he did and handed me a box. 'What is it?' I asked my Teacher. 'It's your confidence,' she said. Suddenly my father reached out to me. My spirit helpers pulled me back quickly. Although he had given me back my confidence he was still not completely healed.

Following this Journey, Catherine's life changed completely. She wrote to me later:

'I had never understood how anyone could want to be alive. I had spent all my adult life wanting to be dead. Now I can see how beautiful, how wonderful, life is. I never knew this before.'

The Land of the Dead is difficult to describe. We can only see what our senses are capable of seeing. We can only interpret what we see in our own ways. We use our senses to understand the world around us and, while we might well be aware that what we sense is a pale reflection of what is, it is the reflection that we have to cope with. Much has been written recently implying that the 'new science', having discovered that the world is not as simple as Newtonian physics might have suggested, is now agreeing with what shamans have 'always known'.

It's a very material way of looking at existence, to feel that everything has to be proved by science before it has any standing. The popular spreading of the idea that physicists now believe in the same things that shamans do is true to neither physics nor shamanism.

Through my experiences and through the experiences of friends and students I have come to certain beliefs concerning death and the Land of the Dead. This is empirical, in that I draw the conclusions that, so far, all the facts I have fit. Occasionally a new fact comes up and I have to change my theories to fit this new fact in. When this happens, I Journey to talk to my Teachers about it. But, so far, there has been remarkable consistency.

When I was young I had a place in my memory that I called 'the green door'. This was more of a green garden gate, actually, made of wood and set into a stone wall that was too high for me to climb. In front of this gate was a shingle beach. No matter how I tried I could never enter through the door. It always remained closed to me. Sometimes I dreamed about this place. Sometimes I would imagine myself there, on the beach. Mostly I was just aware that the green door represented 'home' to me. It was a place to which I longed to find my way back. It took me many years, until I started Journeying, to find out that the green door was a back entrance to the Land of the Dead, and many years more before I realised why I was so attached to it.

Beyond the green door is a lawn, dotted with a few large trees. Beyond the lawn is a Victorian-style building. I said, in the chapter on Soul Retrieval, that to an extent we see things as we expect to see them, that I believe the Orphanage is the same as the Cave of Lost Children. This building, therefore, is one that you might see differently. I call it the Hospital.

The front is imposing. Around the back there are the pipes and vents that you find on a building where the plumbing has been added later. This is where souls that need healing after the experiences of their last life come to be so healed. Among the people that we have known who spent time here are Catherine's father and Helen's mother, Sandra. It seems that the problems that are healed here are mental and emotional ones rather than physical ones. Physical problems disappear once a soul reaches the Land of the Dead. One of the first dead souls that I helped had died after many months battling AIDS-related cancer. During these months he had been hospitalised and bedridden. He did not need the Hospital. What he needed was clear space in which to do the walking, running and dancing he had not been able to do for so long. Christine's uncle, born with severe learning disabilities, lost all traces of his disability once he reached the Land of the Dead.

But my aunt, who had severe mental problems, including schizophrenia, needed a great deal of help after death and she spent over a year (at least, over a year by our time) in the Hospital.

The other group of people who seem to need this kind of healing are those who have died in very traumatic circumstances. Not all of these require help but we have taken souls of murdered children, for example, to the Hospital.

Beyond the Hospital is the rest of the Land of the Dead. Again, there is a great deal of consensus. During workshops where advanced students learn to help the dead we do a Journey to visit the Land of the Dead. This is not a Journey to be undertaken lightly. Shamans all over the world know that, although it is easy to get to the Land of the Dead, it is not always easy to return. One reason for this is that the Land of the Dead is a familiar and welcoming place that our souls have know during the time between incarnations, the place where we are before birth as well as after death. It is a place where we feel at home. It is easy, therefore, for bits of soul to stay there when we Journey. Clearly, this is not a good state of affairs. If we have parts of our soul in the Land of the Dead then they will call to the rest of our soul. We all yearn to be whole. A person with soul in the Land of the Dead is more likely to die by illness, accident or even suicide brought on by a lack of enthusiasm for life. This Journey is only done by experienced Journeyers whose Teachers have agreed that it is appropriate.

'We went to an area of rolling downs. People were walking, picking flowers, talking to each other. My Teacher said they were relaxing – getting accustomed to the place before they started to work.'

'I went to a city of tall white and pastel buildings. I entered a building and came to a room with tall windows. Someone lay, Journeying, with another person sitting there. I asked what was happening. "She's seeking advice from the spirits that will help her plan for her next life, with a counsellor's help. There are many helpers here and many ways of helping," my Teacher said.'

'I was taken on a boat across a sea to some islands. People come here to be alone. Not separate but with themselves. Some for healing and some to prepare for being born soon, I was told.'

'There was a town with a square and a well. The buildings were white, like classical Greece. One was a Library. I was told that I would be able to spent time in the Library when I died.'

'I was on a beach and entered through a green door. Then I was in stillness, peace and quiet, in a lush landscape. I came to a hospital. It was full of people. Very clean and surrounded by gardens.'

The second of these Journeys, the one with the person Journeying, was one of my Journeys. I had come across the fact that in the Hospital some of the healing that takes place is shamanic. That some of the people who work in the Hospital do shamanic Journeys to the spirit realms in order to fetch back soul parts for patients who are missing them. This seems to indicate to me something fundamental about the nature of the Land of the Dead. That it is not a place of pure spirit. This is pretty much against most beliefs, whether they be Christian, one of the eastern religions or modern New Age thinking. But it is what my Teachers tell me when I ask them about it.

> *The Land of Spirit is different from the Land of the Dead, which, like the Land of the Living, is not the Spirit Realms.*

I think that this is why some Teachers can accompany you into the Land of the Dead and others can't. My healing Teacher does not come into the Land of the Dead. I have a special Teacher who works with me there. To contact my healing Teacher while in the Land of the Dead I would have to do a shamanic Journey, as I do here. She does not live there. Recently my Teacher showed me a vision of a mountain. It was steep-sided and flat-topped and on it was another mountain. This also was steep-sided and flat-topped and on it was another mountain. And so on, higher than I could see.

> *'These,' he said, pointing to the lower mountains, 'are the material realms. And these,' pointing to the middle ones, 'are the spirit realms.'*
>
> *'What about those?' I asked, pointing upwards to the highest ones I could see.*
>
> *'Those are beyond the spirit realms,' he said, smiling. 'Most, not all, souls are climbing on the lower mountain slopes. Some slip back occasionally, some stop for longer or shorter rests, some climb steadily upwards. As you climb the mountains of the material realms you go through many lives, learning lessons that will help you to climb further. And you go through many deaths. The Land of the Dead and the Land of the Living are different. The Land of the Dead is less bound to the material than the Land of the Living is. For example, when souls enter the Land of the Dead they often choose to appear as they did in the Land of the Living at a time when they were particularly happy. Then, as they finish dealing with their finished life and move on to planning*

THE LAND OF THE DEAD

their next, they leave behind all appearance of that last life. This being less bound is necessary if you are going to have the wide perspective to plan ahead.

'In the same way, it is necessary for the Land of the Living to be more bound. This enables us to be living in the world fully and to be learning the necessary lessons.

'But they are both in the material realms. They both, for example, work within a perception of time as linear. Of course, we know that time isn't linear, but there are many good, educational reasons to perceive it as such while you are climbing these particular mountains.'

Another Journey that we do on that Dealing with Death workshop is to find out what we will do when we next reach the Land of the Dead. Here are descriptions from some of the Journeys done by students:

'I was shown a book of my life and a book of my life-plan. Then I was left to meditate on the two, reading them and comparing them.'

'I walked through a grey fog. Then I joined a queue of people waiting to go through huge gates. Some were let through. Some were turned back.'

'I sat on a bench in a garden. I was told that this was the start of my healing and learning phase.'

'I worked in a team of three, in the Library, sorting out "ideas".'

'I was told that what I will do depends on what I achieve this lifetime. Two possibilities that were shown to me were working in the storage rooms in the Library or helping souls who pass through the Garden of Choices.'

'The possibilities are wide open. It depends on what I do this lifetime. I was asked, "What do you want to do?"'

'Souls are sorted. Then the past life is reviewed. There is time for relaxation, which is an important part of recuperation.'

'People are met. If they are ill, they go to the Hospital. Then to the Gardens, to rest. They do things that interest them while they decide what to do next.'

'We get help with analysing our lives. Then rest and deciding when and if to return to the Land of the Living.'

'First assessment. Then to the Hospital or to communities in which we will live. To the Garden of Life and the Garden of Life-plans, where we can look back on what we have done and what we had planned to do. In the Garden of Meditation we compare the two. Then we go to the Garden of Choices. Here we can get an overview of our soul's path and have help to plan ahead. Then to the Garden of Relaxation. Finally, to the Garden of Oblivion and the Chute of Life, which takes us back into the Land of the Living.'

As you can see, there is quite a lot of agreement between these accounts. We arrive at the gates to the Land of the Dead. There we are met and, if we are sick, sent to the Hospital. Otherwise we go, often with friends or relatives who have died before us, to communities in which we will live.

Then there is a time of rest. We are helped to review our life and see where and how (or, indeed, if) we achieved those lessons that we set out to learn. There is work that we can do. And there are people to help us plan what we want to achieve next life. Then, when we are ready, we are helped to forget our past and move onwards to be born again into the Land of the Living.

'Why do we have to forget?' we sometimes ask. 'Wouldn't everything be easier if we could only remember what it is that we are supposed to be learning?'

Well, yes, in some ways I suppose it would. But there's a lot to be said for having a clean slate. Suppose, born in the late twentieth century, you could remember that in your last life you had been Adolf Hitler, or a serial killer, or a rapist. Or a victim of any of those. That would have to colour your attitude to life and make it much harder to move on and learn the lessons of your present incarnation.

And if we know exactly what we want to learn, then our actions will be those that we think will best teach us. And we could be wrong. We'd almost certainly miss out on the happy, and not so happy, accidents that happen along the way and may teach us a great deal.

It is a common belief that everything that happens to us in life is something that we consciously chose. I don't agree with this. For a start, there is the callousness that this can engender:

'You can't complain about your life in a wheelchair/concentration camp/war-torn country. You chose it for yourself.'

And – as I have heard from more than one person –

'We mustn't help famine victims. They chose that life.'

Life on our planet just isn't that simple or comfortable. Have you noticed that it isn't the victims of these circumstances who put forward the theory? It's not the famine victim who says, 'Please don't help me. I chose this life.'

Of course we can learn lessons from tragedies. We can learn lessons from anything. But that isn't to say that we planned to learn those lessons. Nor are all lessons good ones. We can learn fear as well as compassion, hate as well as love.

Eventually, during our time in the Land of the Dead, we reach a stage where we are ready to think about our next incarnation. I asked my Teacher about the plans that we make for our next lives.

He took me to a beach, in the Land of the Dead. A figure sat on a stone. I asked it if I could talk to it and it said, 'Anything to help.'

It had the appearance of being in its mid-thirties and had pale skin and fair hair. It was tall and slim and of no discernible sex. I asked it why it was there and it said that very soon, in a few days, it would be born. It was getting itself prepared for that. I asked it what plans it had for the life it was going to lead and it said that it had very few, except to learn how to be focused and to achieve goals. It planned to be born into a poor, black family in New York City. It wanted to have to overcome this background in order to learn. It thought maybe that it would become a doctor or a lawyer. What it became wasn't important. It was in the becoming of it that it would learn. I said that it'd chosen a difficult task and it said that it had done easier things in past lives but this time it needed this challenge. Nothing else was planned. Not sex nor position in family. Not a car crash at eighteen or a lottery win at thirty. Not being alive during a major disaster. Very little, in fact. Just the bare bones of a life focused on overcoming an obstacle.

Sometimes it can be useful to ask our spirits what plans we have made for this life.

'To learn to tell the truth.'
'To learn about laughter.'
'To become part of a community.'
'To maintain a spiritual belief in the face of adversity.'

Several years ago a good friend of ours died, in his twenties. He suffered, since birth, from a particular condition that had caused him a lot of pain and many times we had not expected him to live as long as he did. After his death I visited him to see if I could help him in any way, and I also asked him if he had regrets about his life.

'No,' he said, 'I knew when I was about to be born that this body was damaged and I would not live a long life. But I needed to have those particular people as my parents. It was worthwhile for me, just to be with Mum and Dad.'

The Land of the Dead is the place for the overview of all our lives. It is not usual for an in-depth knowledge of past lives to be with us in the Land of the Living. But, occasionally, there is need to look at our past lives in order to understand or heal our present one. The advantage of asking our spirit helpers rather than using, for example, hypnotic regression, is that they can tell or show us the bits that will most help us. A Journey that I have done with students is, 'What, of my past lives, is it appropriate for my soul to remember now?' But I find Journeys that concentrate on healing rather than on satisfying curiosity of more use. Journeys such as, 'What is the main wound of my past lives and what should I be doing now to heal this wound?' brought forth the following:

'No one listened to me.'
'I believed that I couldn't do things.'
'Separation and loneliness.'
'Being an outcast.'

'How are the gifts of my past lives able to help me now?' also gave some interesting and thought-provoking messages:

'Gifts from past lives come into this one as latent talents.'
'Experiences in past lives give us the tools we need to fix things.'
'The gift I have learned from past lives is courage.'

Earlier in this chapter one of the Journeyers said:

'I joined a queue of people waiting to go through huge gates. Some were let through. Some were turned back.'

It is a dreadful thought that having, at last, reached the Land of the Dead, we might not be let in! I know of only one situation in which this happens. That is when the person has so much soul loss that he or she is disturbed and damaged to the extent that he could damage others – and often has been doing so while alive. I'm not talking here about the damage done in the general hurly-burly of life. We all do harm to others, often without any intention of doing so. I am talking about the serious harm done by child abusers, torturers etc. Wilful harm, done with malice aforethought.

This is not about punishment. The offender is turned away because the Land of the Dead is not a place with the facilities to deal with this type of person, who has to be restrained to prevent harm being done. The situation is rare and, in all cases that I have had anything to do with, has been caused by massive soul loss, often from lifetimes back.

The man had caused much pain during his life. He had been physically and sexually abusive towards his own family and to others and had eventually murdered. When he died, Christine Journeyed to see if she could help prevent him causing suffering during his next incarnation.

I went with my Teacher to the place where I meet souls. I called his name and the figure of a human male appeared. He had long teeth and his fingers were like claws. He sidled closer to me, snarling. My Teacher threw a rope around him and dragged him away.

'I'm taking him to the Void,' he shouted, over his shoulder. 'He needs to be there for a good long time.'

The Void has already been mentioned with regard to soul retrieval. Occasionally souls, both those soul parts that are lost from a living person and those souls that have died, get lost there and have to be rescued. But, for the most part, it is a place for those souls that cannot be contained anywhere else. One spirit Teacher described it thus:

> *'It is bottomless and timeless. The insubstantial are pulled in by accident, but it is there to put souls for healing if their damage is too great for the Hospital to cope with. Inside, there is nothing but yourself to focus on. The healing is slow and deep.'*

The Void is not the only place that the seriously disturbed dead can go. Our client's grandmother had been a controlling and unpleasant woman while alive. Christine went to find her.

> *I was immediately at a place I know in the Lower World. I found that I was dressed formally in my robe and headdress. My Teacher told me to come with him.*
>
> *'We're going hunting,' he said, grimly. 'We will not be persuading, coercing or forgivingly nice. We are in search of a seriously dangerous person.'*
>
> *We ran for miles through a grey land, very misty and full of shifting shapes and odd sounds. Here we walked carefully, looking and listening. Things scuttled away from us as we approached. Then we came to a place where a human figure stood. It was thin, bony. As I neared it turned around quickly. Its mouth was open and it showed fangs. Its hands were claws. It sprang at me but I side-stepped and threw a net, which covered it and held it fast. It screamed and lashed out with claws and spikes on hands, elbows, knees and feet. It bit and slashed at the net with its teeth.*
>
> *'This is the person you seek,' I was told. 'Do not bring her a power animal. She is too ill for that. She will abuse any power that you give her. See how she has been draining power from the living.' My Teacher indicated a purple, pulsing cord fixed to her abdomen. 'Like a leech, but with human understanding, human emotions, human greed.'*
>
> *I asked, 'Should we take her to the Hospital for healing?'*
>
> *'Later,' he said. 'First she must go to the Pit.'*

We dragged her away. She made an awful noise but I was told to ignore it. That was hard. She screamed abuse and threats and cried loudly in pain and fear. It was horrible.

Then we got to a place that was huge and black, lit from the flames of an enormous fire, which spluttered and threw up gouts of flame. I was horrified. It looked as I had always imagined Hell to be. My Teacher made no comment, but threw the net onto the fire. She screamed as the flames consumed her. I stood and watched as the flames ate away at her flesh. Then the fire began to spit out bones. Clean, white bones, into a tidy heap. My Teacher put them into a bag and led me away.

This time we went up and over the Rainbow Bridge and into the Land of the Dead. We turned right and walked softly and carefully until we reached the Hospital, where we went up the steps and to the reception desk.

A woman greeted us and said, briskly, 'We've been expecting you. Go with the nurse and do as she says.'

We followed the nurse along a corridor to a bed in a ward. The nurse told me to put the bones onto the bed. I did this and then watched in amazement as the bones rearranged themselves into a skeleton. As I watched, a haze began to glow around the bones, like an aura.

'As she heals and solidifies into a person, her power animal will join her,' said the nurse.

I asked the nurse if the woman had felt pain in the fire.

'No,' she said, 'how could she? She is spirit.'

I felt somewhat comforted and left with my Teacher.

But there are others who do not reach the Land of the Dead at all.

Many people have the ability to contact the spirits of the dead who are stuck on this plane and are able to say to them:

'Look around you. Look around until you see the light. Do you see the light? Now go towards it.'

As I say, the Universe is a loving place. This works – as long as there are no complications. If the spirit is here, stuck on this plane, able and willing to go to the light, then this will happen.

I'm not suggesting here that the world is split into two where light equals good and dark equals bad. That is far too simple. But if spirits are stuck they are often stuck in a place of mist and greyness.

The light shining across the Rainbow Bridge is not a 'pure, white light', but that of sunshine and daylight. I once visited the spirit realms to find everything dark and I asked my Teacher why this was so. Very patiently, as if speaking to a loved but not very bright child, he said, 'It's dark because it's night-time. Everything needs rest.'

If the spirit is stuck somewhere between this plane and the Land of the Dead, so that, no matter how psychic you may be, you are not aware of it because it's somewhere else, or if the spirit doesn't want to go to the Land of the Dead for whatever reason, or if the spirit is so bound up and confused that it cannot think of going on until it is sorted out, then no amount of sending to the light is going to work. Something else needs to be done. If nothing is done then the soul can reincarnate from this in-between place, without having ever been healed from the traumas of the last life, without having had a chance to review the life just led and without getting the chance to plan for the next life.

The big strength of shamanism in situations such as this is the ability to go in search of the spirit when it is no longer in this plane. We are not calling the spirit to us; we are actually going to look for it. And we are going to look for it accompanied by our Teachers and spirit helpers, with all the skill, knowledge, love and compassion that they can bring with them.

When people are alive they are here, on this plane. When they are dead they are in the Land of the Dead. I wish it were that simple. Of course, many souls move without complications from the Land of the Living to the Land of the Dead. I have known several who have done so. My brother-in-law's mother, for example, who was elderly and had come to the end of a long life, stayed at the waiting place only long enough to be polite. She thanked Christine for our concern, said that as soon as she had died she 'had remembered the way' and went away over the Rainbow Bridge very happily. A television personality who was a gardener and a deeply spiritual, although not necessarily religious, man had already gone. There was no need for any help. According to my Teacher the very old and the very young can usually remember the way.

But some souls do get stuck. And for many reasons. One of the most common is simple confusion. I remember a man, a devout

Christian, who knew that he was dying of cancer. He made all the arrangements necessary to tie up loose ends before he died, he saw his friends and bade them goodbye, he had the Last Rites. He died. When Christine went to check on him he was confused. He had spent so long concentrating on what he should do in life that he had spared no thought for what would happen next. Of course, he was simply lost. Once he had been spoken to and reassured he could be pointed in the right direction and off he went. Another man, a film actor, had no idea what to do after death. 'No script, you see, my dear,' he said.

Others are lost because the mode of death has been traumatic and, often, sudden. A particularly heart-rending type is children who have been murdered. That's always a dreadful situation to have to deal with. We hear news reports on the television and go to our spirits to see if we can help. One of the saddest aspects is not being able to let the parents know that at least their child has reached the Land of the Dead safely and has been greeted by loved ones there. The last thing a bereaved parent, who might for all we know be a member of a religion that would regard shamanism as devil-worship, wants is for some crank to contact them saying, 'Little Jimmy is fine now and sends his love.'

Some souls are confused because they were ill, drunk or drugged when they died. This includes those who were taking medication in hospitals. Any confusion at the time of death seems to do it. This often happens with suicides. Only the most determined are able to kill themselves with no regrets whatsoever, with no 'I've changed my mind,' just as the last minute has gone. That dichotomy of wanting to die and, at the same time, not wanting to – and both can be strong in a suicide – can lead to soul-splitting and confusion. Those who do, single-mindedly, want to die are often in no fit state to find their way to the Land of the Dead, anyway. I have never come across a suicide who managed to reach the gates of the Land of the Dead without help.

So what happens to these souls? This is another question that students ask their Teachers on the workshop that deals with death. Here are some of the answers they have received:

They get stuck. Some fade out of existence, some fall into the Void, some get reborn from the in-between place.'

They are stuck and need help. They are alone. Some play out endless scenes. Some draw energy from the living by haunting or possession. Sometimes they get help but a lot don't.'

They become wandering souls, some not knowing that they are dead. Some have soul parts missing and these can fade or be sucked into the Void. Souls can die if they are not saved.'

We come into life with pre-determined goals. But some souls are knocked seriously off course. If they die before they get back on track then they become lost. Their inner compass has gone wrong.'

Some become convinced they should still be in the Land of the Living. They haunt and possess.'

Christine asked her Teacher to help her understand the destination of souls when they die.

My Teacher took me to a high place and we sat and talked.

The essence of a person, the personality, is the part that you psychopomp,' he said.

The physical body has a spirit but, without the essence, it cannot be activated. However, if the body is ill-treated, then, under some circumstances, it can be reactivated – ghouls and zombies and so on are reactivated physical remains.

The essences reach the "Edge Land", the half-way place, and there parts of souls which have left through trauma and got lost may reattach themselves, attracted like iron filings to a magnet. Not often, though.

Sometimes part of a soul can be left in Ordinary Reality, "haunting" the house by re-enacting the trauma that caused it to be lost in the first place, for centuries, until it fades into the walls and becomes part of the spirit of everything.

The spirit of the physical body remains until the body decays. This takes a very long time with modern embalming techniques. For a while the body continues to "live" but eventually that fades. Finally, after the body has gone, the spirit returns to the earth as part of the spirit of everything.'

When Christine first told me of this Journey I was rather confused by the words, *'The essence of a person, the personality, is the part that you psychopomp,'* because I would have thought that the essence of a person was the immortal part, the soul, while the personality was the mortal part, the part that belongs to each incarnation. After thinking carefully about this and asking my own Teacher about it I have realised that, although it is, indeed, the essence or soul that is psychopomped, that part has the personality of the last life still because, at that point, being stuck, that life is all that can be remembered.

So, many souls make it without problems to the Land of the Dead. Others get stuck and have to be helped. The confusion that souls feel, that keeps them stuck, is the result of a lack of connection at the time of death. And, as in healing, the best solution to a lack of connection is a power animal retrieval. No one can be disconnected when their power animal is beside him or her.

Martin asked Christine to help Susie, who had died in a road accident.

I met my Teacher at the usual place. A young woman was standing there, looking lost.

'Hello,' I said, 'are you Martin's friend, Susie?'

She looked surprised.

'Yes,' she said, 'I was out with my friends. What happened?'

I explained about the accident and she became distraught.

'No! No! I don't want to be dead! I've too much to do, too much to live for!' She flung herself at me. I tried to comfort her but felt totally inadequate. My Teacher stepped forward, there was a loud fluttering noise and a huge peacock came.

'He's for you,' I said, 'to help you and to love you. Now it's time to join your friends over the Bridge.'

She looked up at the Rainbow Bridge, much happier since the peacock was with her. At the gates to the Land of the Dead I could see her family waiting for her. The peacock led the way over the Bridge, his tail spread proudly. She followed him.

A young child had been murdered. This is always a terrible thing, both for the child and for the family left behind. Christine Journeyed to see if she could help him.

> *The little boy was in a very distressed state, frightened and in pain, stuck in the moment of death. My Teacher held him gently and we all proceeded towards the Land of the Dead. We didn't enter by the main gate but skirted the Land until we reached the back entrance to the Hospital. There we were met and taken into a long ward filled with rows of beds. Beside each was a chair on which sat an animal. We were taken towards an empty bed, beside which sat a mallard. The little boy smiled, for the first time since I'd seen him. He held out his arms, and cried:*
>
> *'Oh, Duck! I have missed you!'*

The 'usual place' is where Christine's Teacher and her spirit helpers bring lost souls, for her to help. Occasionally she has to go searching. People who have died suddenly might not actually go anywhere. One young man, murdered in a pub brawl, was found some months later, still outside the pub, trying to find his way home to his mother and totally unaware that he was dead.

> *I went to my spirits and said that I was looking for Richard's soul.*
>
> *My Teacher said, 'Come, then. We have a long Journey to make.'*
>
> *We flew up and crossed the skies until we came to land in a town at night. We were outside a pub. It was crowded and noisy. Light spilled out of the windows. The pavement was wet, shining in the streetlights. I noticed a shadowy figure and walked up to it. It was a young man.*
>
> *'Are you Richard?' I asked.*
>
> *He seemed puzzled, so I asked again. He brightened.*
>
> *'Yes! Richard. Who are you?'*
>
> *I told him and said that his mother had sent me.*
>
> *'My mother? I've been trying to go home to her, but I can't seem to find my way away from here.' He looked distressed. 'What happened?'*
>
> *I told him that there had been a fight. He was now dead, stabbed with a knife. He was horrified. Then furious. Then desperate. My spirits brought forward an ostrich and Richard immediately calmed down.*

'I understand now, but I must see Mum again – to say goodbye.'

My Teacher took us all to a house in the suburbs and we landed in the garden. My Teacher called out to the soul of Richard's mother and, when she appeared, Richard spoke to her. He said thank you and goodbye and that he was sorry to have upset her. Then we took him to the Rainbow Bridge and left him and his ostrich to go up and across. He waved once and then was gone.

I'd like to end this chapter on a high note, with a couple of Journeys that I did recently. Diane had been to see me to have a soul retrieval and the part that I brought back for her had been with her father, Andrew, who had died some years previously. He was stuck and I was able to take him to the Hospital. Diane went home and told her mother about what had happened and, about a month later, Diane's mother, Jean, came to see me. I went back to the Land of the Dead to talk to Andrew.

I went straight to my Teacher and she dressed me in a black robe and gave me my staff. This is a sure sign that I need to be official when I go to the Land of the Dead. I accompanied my Death Teacher, floating beside him. At the gates to the Land of the Dead I knocked and announced myself. There was a great deal of activity inside and a young man came up to the gates and told me that there was a huge parade going on.

'We'll have to get to the Hospital by a back way,' he said.

He took me through gardens and other buildings until we reached the Hospital, where he left me with the receptionist. She took me to a window and let me look through it at Andrew. He was lying on the bed, looking pale but smiling and chatting to a tall man who stood by the bed. His power animal sat on the chair beside him. I asked who the man was and was told that this was Andrew's grandfather.

The receptionist said, 'We took three soul parts out of Andrew, souls that he shouldn't have had.'

She peered closely at three boxes on the shelf nearby.

'This one is his wife's. We'll keep it safe for her until you come to collect it. This one is his sister and this one …' She looked at the box more closely. 'This one seems to be a dog. Goodness! That one can be dealt with easily enough. That doesn't need you! Bring the bit of him that his wife has and bring something to carry her soul part back in.' I did an extraction of Andrew's soul part from Jean and put the part into a stone. Then I Journeyed, with the stone and with my soul carrier crystal, back to the Land of the Dead.

Once again I had to dress in my robe to go to the Land of the Dead. When I got there almost everyone seemed to be in a central square. They were cheering and obviously very happy. I was met by the same young man and taken by the same back way. I asked him what was going on. He smiled at me, radiantly, and said, 'It's someone who has come back, who we thought was lost. Someone that your world thinks of as a monster, a Hitler or Jack the Ripper. He was lost for a long time and then was in the Void for a long time. Finally he has been in the Hospital having healing and counselling. But now he is well and is one of us again. We are so happy.'

I went into the Hospital and handed over the stone with Andrew's soul part in it. The receptionist gave it to a man dressed in a robe that was covered with feathers and bones. I asked who he was and was told:

'He is one of our shamans. One who works here as you do in your world.'

The shaman laid the stone on Andrew and rattled and sang the soul part back into him. It spread through him in a golden glow. Then the shaman handed me back the stone.

'It's empty now. Wash it in the usual way.'

The receptionist gave me the box that contained Jean's soul part. I asked was there anything I could do to help Andrew's sister. I was told no, not unless she asked for help in the future. However, her soul part was safe and the next time she found her way to the Land of the Dead it would be re-united with her. I brought Jean's soul part back to her.

CHAPTER SIX

ELEMENTAL SPIRITS

Not all shamanic work is healing and psychopomping. Many of us work with the elements of earth, air, fire and water. I'm sure that we can all picture in our heads the elemental spirits of fire, earth, air and water. Fire is wild, fast and furious. Passionate. Liable to burn us if we get too careless. Earth is stolid and strong. Water is emotional and loving and Air playful. Or whatever our tradition or memories of fairy-tales has taught us. And, of course, all this is true. But when we reach out and touch the elementals, when we really get to know them, it isn't quite that simple. We may well be in for a surprise.

Let's look at Fire first. Look around you now and think of fire. Fire gives warmth and light. Maybe you have an open fire, as I have, or a gas fire. Then the flames are easy to see. But fire is present in the warmth from a central heating radiator. It is in a light bulb. And, of course, in a candle flame. It is in the sun, from which we all get sustenance. Without the heat and light of the sun nothing could live. All the ways that we have of producing light and heat owe their origins to the sun.

I hope that you have not had the terrible experience of being badly damaged by fire. But all of us will have burned our fingers at some time. Fire teaches us to be careful. And it can teach us many other things as well. The following quotations are from fire spirits. Some of these will be from the spirit of an individual flame, maybe the candle flame that the Journeyer was sitting with prior to Journeying. Others, in Journeys that were done around a bonfire, will be from the spirit of that fire.

'A warm heart is a happy heart. Keep a warm heart.'

'I am a volcano. I am a gas lamp. I am the life in you.'

'Feed the fire with new experiences. This is life – change and uncertainties.'

'I am creativity. I am in everyone.'

These are a few of the things students have been told when they have been to ask the fire for a teaching. The following is in reply to the question:

'What is the relevance of fire to me?'

'Clarity, integrity, direction. I am the spark of life within everything. I give purpose. I am in passion and in compassion. Without the fire of the sun there is no warmth, no light, no life. I make the sap rise in the stems and the life-energy rise in your body. Work with me to burn through your life, leaving only truth, clarity, direction, love. Be with me. Work with me and get to know me better. I temper the steel and burn away the dross, leaving the clear crystal of truth.'

Fire is fragile, easily extinguished by water, earth or air. Each flame is short-lived, striving to stay alive by devouring anything in its path that it can live on. And, because it is short-lived, it also strives to reproduce. So, if the conditions are right, one flame gives life to many others. Any many flames together can be very dangerous to those on whom fire can feed – humans, trees, buildings. But fire itself is not angry or vindictive. It just is. We should not look to fire for a moral sense. It does what fire does.

What about Air? Air spirits are as essential to our existence as are the fire spirits or, indeed, all of the elements. My students and I asked the spirits to help us to experience the air inside us.

'I was aware of my own breath. And I was aware of the landscape breathing in and out as well. Air is the breath of life. We speak of "the last breath" or "the dying breath" but after that air is still there, in the body, in the pores. Air is in death as it is in all things.'

'Air spirits are like eddies in the water. The spaces all around us are air. Air is the reason things are able to move.'

'Air bathes us both inside and out.'
'Air is in everything. It is the gap between.'
'We only see it when it is moving.'
'We can only hear the drumbeat because air carries the sound.'

Take a moment to concentrate on your breath. This is the most immediate way that we experience air. The whole practice of breathing is automatic and we have to pause and focus on our breath to be aware that we are breathing. But we would soon become aware if there were no air to breathe. For a very short while. With no food we can live for many days. With no water, for a few days. But without air we can only survive for a few minutes. And our brains would be affected first. We need air in order to think. Air gives us clarity. We asked the air spirits to show us what it was like to be part of the air.

'I laughed and danced in the fire, making the sparks swirl. The hawthorn was full of energy; blue, purple, white. Breath, lungs, blood. Wheee! That was great!'

'Like a rollercoaster, around cars and tents and through hedges. Life rushing along, avoiding worries, at break-neck speed. Isn't it great?'

'Flying quickly, low to the ground, through the grass. Wind flows. Like fire or water there are tongues that fly up and die down. It's in everything. It's in the beating of the drum, in breathing. It flows as a subtle energy through all things growing.'

'The drum vibration was red, orange, yellow. Everything was breathing in blue and out green.'

'Always moving, never stopping.'

'Wind played with the sounds, batting them around. When we were just talking there were some spirits around. As soon as we started drumming there were hundreds coming to join in.'

'Pete's tractor was in front of us. We went through the air cleaner and inlet manifold, through the piston and out of the exhaust.'

Air told me:

'I am everywhere. Without me you could not breathe, you could not live. I am fierce and I blow away the cobwebs, leaving

clarity behind. Leaving behind only those things that matter enough to hang on to, only those things that value themselves enough to hang on!'

The earth supports us. She is all around us. Not just 'in the country' or 'out in nature', but everywhere. The cities are built on earth. They are built of stones dug from the earth or bricks made of the clay of the earth. Metal, glass and plastic are all, ultimately, from the earth. In a sense we are all children of the earth. She gives birth to us and nurtures us from her own body. She is the mother of us all. She has given us food, shelter and support since the day we were born.

It is easy to find the earth outside of us. We look and it is there. Let us try to find the earth that is within us. Here are some of the things that the spirits of the earth told us when we asked them to help us experience the earth within us.

'The earth within you is unconditional living.'
'We are one with all earth.'
'We are beings that are made of clay. We are particles of stone in water, we are land bearing trees, we are crystals. We are whatever is tough and protective. The earth is bone, rock, flesh and mud.'
'Skeleton, skin, molecules. Without me your spirit would have no form. The universe would have no form.'
'I feel pressure in the earth. Rocks and mud and people, everything is made of the same earth. I experienced being a sedimentary layer. I was eroded and then built up into other rocks. We are made of minerals; calcium, iron, zinc. We are earth.'
'Earth is the means by which you enter this physical body. It holds you to this place.'
'I am the earth. I am a mobile rock. I am of, from and shall return to, the earth. A mudball with a bit of a brain for a short time.'

Stones are an obvious piece of earth. From tiny quartz crystals to huge granite megaliths, not forgetting sacred mountains, human beings have honoured and praised stones. I asked students to visit the spirit of an individual stone to find out from it what being a stone was like. The overwhelming sensations were those of connection and of being.

'We are internally connected by energy all over the earth. Energy flows everywhere.'

'A stone is connected to every other mineral that touches the earth.'

'The stones vibrated. I couldn't breathe. I was drawn down into the stones, spiralled out and then back to earth in a beacon of love. Everything is connected.'

'A stone is old. Days, years and seasons pass. The stone accumulates wisdom. It is so old that it is not waiting any more, it has not patience any more, just being.'

And finally we visit water. Every now and again I come across someone who tells me that he or she cannot drink water. So what do they drink? Tea, coffee, orange juice, milk or Coca-Cola. And what is the main ingredient of all these? That's right, water. Water is, like fire, air or earth, necessary for life. And like fire, air and earth, water is everywhere.

'I watched three drops of water on a blade of grass. Everything is cyclical. Water is the blood of life. Honour all the elements.'

'Water is there even when it is not obvious.'

'Water is. You can understand this intellectually. But, like water in a container, you need to burst the boundaries in order to really know it.'

'Water is everywhere. Be like water. It has no expectations, it just is.'

'Connection, change and flow.'

'Drink water for purity.'

'Joy is even where you don't expect it. Dance when you see water.'

'Life needs water and water needs life.'

'There is water everywhere.'

'Cleanse, move, connect, adapt, sustain life.'

'Get out of the rain.'

This last one may seem like strange advice to come from a water spirit. But when we ask the spirits a question we get an answer for ourselves, personally, that is related to our own needs and level of learning. The student concerned had been working very hard, making life difficult for herself out of a sense of duty. She interpreted the message as meaning, 'You don't have to be uncomfortable. It's okay to pamper yourself a little.' A different person, with different needs, might have been told something like, 'Go and stand in the rain.'

Water is the component that makes our blood liquid. Water is the reason that our blood flows around our bodies. Water is the way that nutrients feed our organs. It is in saliva and in the juices that digest our food. It enables our bodies to rid themselves of waste. Water is part of us.

All these elements are part of ourselves, our environments and our lives. We need a balance of them. This isn't as simple as saying that such and such a ratio of water to earth is needed by all of us, as nutritionists can about the ratio between potassium and sodium. We have to be in balance, not only with our bodies, but also with our environments. Each area has different energies and balances. Maybe one place has a natural excess of water, another of fire. Everywhere is different, just as deserts are different from temperate coastlines, although each may have sand. And we are all different, with different needs at different times of our lives. Sometimes we can sense what we need. It isn't hard, if we are thirsty, to work out that we need water or, if we are bitterly cold, that some fire will help. But sometimes it is harder to work out what we need. If we feel tired and lethargic we might be able to work out that we probably don't need more earth, but what do we need?

Philip had come to see me because he had been ill for a long time with mental problems, manifesting as an inability to mix with other people. In company he was subject to panic attacks and, because he could not bring himself to travel on public transport, I drove to his home in West Yorkshire to collect him and to take him back. It had taken a great deal of effort and courage for him to come to see me at all. We worked together for three days as I taught him to contact his own helper spirits and to ask their advice. Gradually, he began to feel better. Of course, it had taken him many months to get to the stage of being so ill. He was not going to recover completely in only a few days, but he was given a structure in which he could learn to be well. Towards the end of the three days I went to ask my Teacher for advice on what further I could do for Philip.

'He must connect,' she said. 'He should go to the library when he gets home and ask for their list of local activities. He should chose one that is not based on cumulative knowledge or skill, one where he won't feel that he has let himself down if he misses a week.

'He must not expect to be well until next summer [this was November] *but on the Summer Solstice he should take a picnic to the park and have a celebration with his spirits – a celebration of being well.*

'And his home is not helping. The energies are unbalanced. Check them when you take him back.'

I told all this to Philip and asked if I could check over his home, a bedsit in a larger house. He agreed and when we got there he sat on the bed and watched as I first rattled and then Journeyed.

The house spirit came. I greeted it, a pale blue androgynous figure, with hair and gown that appeared to be made of smoke.

'I've come to ask how Philip's room can contribute to his recovery,' I said.

The figure smiled and touched my face with tendrils of smoke.

'There is too much earth and water here for good health. The room needs fire and air. Tell Philip to open the window for a few minutes every day. And tell him to light a candle once a week.'

Philip agreed that he would do this and I left. I received a card from him a few months later. He accepted that it would take a while – 'until the Summer Solstice,' I reminded him – before he felt completely better, but he was already making great strides. He was working as a volunteer for the RSPCA and really enjoying his contact with other people who cared about the same things as he did. And his room was feeling quite different – 'Pleasant and comfortable.' It had always made him feel as if he were a temporary visitor before.

Liz was a primary school teacher in a small, country school. She liked her job but didn't get on with one particular teacher. It was not that her colleague was a bad person or a poor teacher in any way, but they simply rubbed each other up the wrong way. Liz was intelligent enough to realise that this was her problem as much as it was her colleague's and since she could only change herself, no one else, she asked me if my spirits had any advice for her.

'Too much fire in the classroom,' said my Teacher. 'Balance it with the other three elements.'

I advised Liz, like Philip, to open her window at least once a day, no matter what the weather or temperature. If this sounds drastically uncomfortable, I am not suggesting having the windows wide all day through a gale. Ten minutes, after all the children have gone home, would suffice. In addition, I suggested a pot plant in the room. Plants are common enough in classrooms to excite no comment and the compost in the pot provides earth. A small watering can, full of water for watering the plant, provides water. The three added elements balanced the excess of fire in the room, which was causing both Liz and her colleague trouble.

They are not the best of friends. They have too little in common for that to come about without a great deal of effort on both sides. But the other teacher no longer 'rubs Liz up the wrong way'.

Barry and Elaine were retired, and put their lack of energy down to age. I suggested that I look at the house and see what I could do. The heavy stillness made me think that there was too much earth in the house but, of course, I checked with my spirit helpers before I did anything.

'Yes,' my Teacher agreed, 'too much earth. But also not enough water.'

Following her instructions I opened both the front and back doors. Then I walked in at the front door and, sprinkling water from a bowl as I went, walked through the house and out of the back door. I did this three times. Then I took a handful of earth from the garden. I scattered this earth on the moor on my way home.

Barry and Elaine had another problem with their house that was solved very quickly. The house had been built with an integral

garage. Barry and Elaine rarely used their front door, instead entering the house through the garage, which brought them straight into
the kitchen at the back of the house. This meant that the energies,
which run between the front and back doors in almost all houses,
were being blocked.

There are many ways of unblocking energy. This is only one of
them. I rattled between the two doors, singing a song that my
Teacher had given me, until I had attracted the attention of the spirits. Then, when I had their full attention, I showed them the way in
which the energies could flow through the house even with one
door not in use.

Neither Barry nor Elaine are young. They are not going to find
the energy suddenly to run up stairs without a thought. But they are
finding life a little brighter and nowhere near so tiring.

We first noticed how run-down and depressed the Yorkshire seaside
town was when we were looking for a house in North Yorkshire. In
every other town we walked into estate agents' offices and were met
with smiles and queries:

'Can I help you?'

'What kind of property are you looking for?'

In this town we visited half a dozen estate agents. In none were
we greeted. The sales assistants did not even look up. It was as if
they had given up all hope of ever selling another house.

We finally found our house and, after a while, began looking for
venues in which to teach shamanic workshops. We found a few in
very pleasant parts of Yorkshire but were never able to find any
success in this particular town. We booked workshops there, one a
year. We have had to cancel them all. Now, I don't want to pretend
that cancelling workshops is rare. As anyone who runs them can tell
you, it happens. But this was every workshop in the town – and very
few elsewhere. We had had a lot of interest. People telephoned – but
did not book. When we held workshops in Malton or York people
from this town would enquire:

'Can't you do one nearer? Malton's thirty miles away!'

Meanwhile, people were coming from Manchester, Doncaster,
Hull and Sheffield, occasionally from further afield. It seemed as if a

strange lethargy had overtaken the entire town. Eventually it got through to us that something was wrong and Christine, who had lived in the town when she was young, went to visit the spirits of the place.

I went across country with my Teacher and landed at the castle.
My Teacher stood protectively in front of me and all the rest of my spirit helpers ringed me around.

I felt the spirits of the place come in a huge rush of anger and despair. Spirits swirled, coalesced and separated, all keening a high-pitched song of grief and lament.

'Too much change, too much change.'

'Nothing the same as it was.'

'Not fair. Nobody asked us.'

I asked how I could help them. They were scathing in response.

'You can do NOTHING, NOTHING! You never do anything! You say you will, but you don't. Don't have time. Don't get around to it. Why should we believe you when you say you'll help?'

Startled and rather disturbed, I turned to my Teacher for help. He looked at me.

'Well, there's an element of truth in that,' he said. 'You do have good intentions and you do get side-tracked. But a lot of this is their anger and unhappiness speaking. Would you help if you could? If you knew what to do to make things right, would you do it?'

I nodded.

He went on, 'Come up here to the castle in Ordinary Reality. Bring some water that has been potentised with the spirit of Rose Quartz and give it to the spirits here. Spend some time with the place. Then go home and Journey again.'

I came back.

We did as Christine had been told. I spoke to the spirit of the Rose Quartz crystal that helps me and he was happy to potentise the water. Then we had a trip to the coast, climbed the hill to the castle and sat there with the grass and the wind on the cliff top. We poured out the water onto the ground, voicing our intention to help and asking the spirits to accept our gift. Then we came home and Christine Journeyed again.

I went with my spirits to the castle. The local spirits were wait-
ing. They seemed much calmer, touched and pleased with our
gift and much more willing to talk to me.

'Visit more often, and bring gifts to other parts of the town,'
they said.

Then they showed me the town cemetery where my mother is buried.
The stone was clean and well cared for – living so close, I can visit
regularly.

'When you clean the stone you clean others in spirit, all the neglected
ones, all the uncared-for ones. Keep hers shining and it makes a differ-
ence. There is other work to do in the town but these two things, the
grave and the gifts, are for you to do.'

Following that Journey of Christine's it sounded as if there was
work for me to do there, as well. So I went to check.

My Teacher took me to the headland, drew a circle around me
and announced that only one spirit should talk to me at a time.
After a lot of whispering and arguing an old man stepped forward
and agreed, grudgingly, that, by leaving the water, I had done all
right so far,

'... but there's plenty more to do, you know.'

I asked what needed doing next. He mentioned a bridge that, until
recently, when high fencing had been put up, had been a popular place
for those wishing to kill themselves to jump from.

'The fences stop energy. Many of the souls of the suicides are
still trapped there and that blocks the energy as well, but mainly it's
the fences.'

To me, as a human, it seemed pretty terrible that these souls,
unhappy enough to kill themselves in the first place, should still be
trapped in the place of their death, but, as a land spirit, he was far
more concerned about the fences. I put aside my concerns to return to
later, and asked what I could do, since taking down the fences wasn't
an option.

'It needs two feathers under the bridge, one on each side of the road.
Then take your rattle and walk down the hill, under the bridge,
rattling all the way, until you are standing in the sea.'

I did as I had been told. The two feathers were waiting for me outside the house when I went to look. Feathers are often used for subtle things such as directing or detecting energy. It is possible to hold a feather lightly, maybe from a thread, and, by watching the movements of the feather, 'read' where the energy is more sluggish, or where it moves faster. Part of this is because feathers are designed to feel and manipulate energy, as they help a bird to fly. This could well be why I find wing feathers best for this kind of work. But also there is always the intention of the work. If I put a feather under a bridge with the intention that it will help energies to flow past it, I know that this will work because my spirits have said that it will. We both took another trip to the coast. While Christine did her work, I clambered up the earthen banks beneath the bridge and positioned the feathers. Then I took my rattle and started from above the bridge. As I started to rattle and to walk I was feeling rather self-conscious but, as I became aware of the spirits around me, this wore off and I found a spirit-given song rising to my lips. I walked down the hill, rattling and singing to the energy spirits of the route down to the sea. I could see and feel them all around me as I went. When I reached the beach I paused in the walking and rattling, but not the singing, long enough to remove my shoes and socks. Then I continued until I was standing in the sea. The spirits rushed past me and on into the waves and I felt the song leave me. I stopped rattling and came back to Ordinary Reality.

Much of the problem seemed to be that recent additions to the town, the bridge fences and a new road that cut across the routes down to the sea, had disrupted the energies' sense of where to flow.

If it sounds strange that energy could be disrupted so easily, the answer is in the intention. In putting up the fences the intention had been to block – albeit potential suicides rather than energy – and with the road, the intention had been for the flow of traffic to cut across the old route, leading through traffic, and unintentionally energy, away from the crowded coast itself.

We visited once a month and each month I rattled and sang a different route to the sea. Always I found that I was singing the same song, and always I was accompanied by hordes of spirits until, at last, I stood ankle-deep in the sea.

After four months I asked my Teacher how it was going.

He took me high to look over the town. The four routes I had cleared
shone in golden streams. Energy was pouring along them. Further
inland were some dark, blocked areas, one in a suburb, one at the ceme-
tery, a few others that either need clearing or re-balancing.

These other areas are an on-going project. The suburban shops
needed water. I walked around outside them sprinkling water from
a bowl and singing. It always surprises me how few people seem to
notice when I do things like this. The cemetery had in it several
shining, clear spots – one of which was Christine's mother's grave.
These were the areas that are kept clean and cared for, neither
neglected nor blocked by too much outpouring of emotion. My job
here was to link up these areas by putting flowers on specific graves
that my Teacher chose, all of them neglected and all between forty
and seventy years old. My Teacher tells me that fifty years is a suitable time for a grave to be tended. Some people ask me why, when
the soul has already departed, there is any need to tend a grave at
all, let alone for fifty years. I have said before that I believe that
everything has a spirit. That includes the dead body. There are many
beliefs about the soul from around the world and one that is
common in shamanic cultures is that, while the soul goes to the
Land of the Dead, something else, that I will call the spirit, stays in
the body. It has some of the memories and personality of the
departed soul, but is often more petulant and greedy, greedy for
experiences and attention. Gradually, over the next fifty years, the
spirit will fade. It will lose the sense of individuality and will become
a spirit of the land. Christine visits her mother's grave every couple
of weeks, to wash the stone, leave flowers and also to talk to her. To
let her know how the family are getting on and what the weather is
like. In many parts of the world the spirits of dead bodies are known
to cause trouble if they are not looked after properly. In China there
is a yearly festival to placate the 'Hungry Ghosts', those who have
no relatives to tend their graves or who have no graves. Otherwise,
feeling neglected, they may try to attract attention by breaking
things, setting fires or other acts of damage. This, I believe, is one
of the causes of poltergeists.

Christine had been told to take gifts to other parts of the town.

These took the form of stones, specially selected from places outside the town, which Christine then Journeyed to, to ask their permission. They were to be taken to specific places within the town, three of them islands in ornamental lakes – of which the town has several. She did this once a month for six months. After the first three occasions she Journeyed to ask her Teacher if the gifts had been acceptable to the local spirits.

He came and we flew together to the town, to where I'd thrown the stone yesterday, onto the island. There were lots of spirits there, beaming happily.

'You are doing well. The energy is changing quite perceptibly. You are setting up a chain reaction and after a few more months it will be able to change by itself. Thank you. Well done.'

My Teacher asked me how I'd felt when the stone hit the island.

'Different,' I said. 'Right. As if a weight had been lifted.'

My Teacher asked me to look at the site carefully. I did so.

'It seems more solid,' I said, 'more grounded.'

He nodded. 'Jane is showing the energies where to go. You are grounding the "flights of fancy". So far, all the places you have dealt with are tourist places, not of the town, and therefore not so grounded. Now you must look at places of the town. Put the next stone into the flower tub on the main street.'

'Which one?' I asked, for there are at least a dozen.

'You'll know it,' he said (and, indeed, I did), 'this is to link the "fanciful" town with the "mundane" town.'

One more thing needed doing. I could not forget the poor trapped souls at the bridge. Usually it is Christine who works with souls of the dead, but I was the one who had been told about it.

I was dressed in my black coat and hat and I rode the horse that helps me when I need to make an imposing figure. My Teacher was with me but said that the souls would not be able to see him, only me. I held my staff.

We rode to the bridge and my Teacher showed me where I'd put the feathers. They were glowing. Then he told me to whistle for the souls.

Many people arrived, looking bewildered and lost. Some were squashed and broken. All looked harrowed. My Teacher saw my expression and said, matter-of-factly, 'That's what happens to someone when they jump off a bridge.'

I whistled again, then began to ride. They followed me up, into the sky, my spirits rounding them up like sheep. When we came to the Rainbow Bridge that leads to the Land of the Dead, Horse and I hovered beside it. The souls walked up, still herded. From out of the mist power animals came, one for each person. As the animals joined them, each person seemed to recover somewhat, standing straighter and looking happier. Just inside the gates they were greeted by people with clipboards who directed them further.

As I stood and watched I found myself wondering if I would recognise any of them from newspaper reports I had read. Was one of them the school friend of Christine's who had died in her early twenties?

My Teacher said, 'Don't pick out any individual one. Don't look anyone in the eyes.'

There were dozens.

He said, 'Towards the end they were averaging about one a year.' I remembered, against my will, the last case and he said, sharply, 'Don't look! Just remember. Not everyone wanted to die and some changed their minds when it was too late!'

The last few went through the gates, which clanged shut.

As you can see, a lot of our work with the land involves element-balancing. Not everything, of course. We do extractions and soul retrievals for the land, or for plants, in very much the same way as we do for humans or for animals. But many places are elementally out of balance and need help because of it.

Remember Philip? A few months later he moved from his bedsit to his own small flat. The flat had four rooms; a sitting room, a bedroom, a bathroom and a kitchen. When I asked my Teacher what needed doing there, he said:

'It is a lovely flat. Philip will be happy here. But we will make it even safer and more secure for him. There are four rooms. Tell him to dedicate a room to each element. The bathroom is an obvious

choice for water. Tell him to decorate in blues and greens. Have shells for decoration. The cooker is in the kitchen. This is the best choice for fire. Use warm colours and make it a cheerful, vibrant room. The sitting room should be for Air. Have the windows open whenever possible, with curtains that can billow in the breeze. Burn incense so that the air is sweet-smelling. In the bedroom is Earth. Think of badgers' earths and foxes' dens. A place of safety to come to after the bustle of the day. A grounded place of recuperation. This is his private space, for him alone.'

We don't all live alone in a four-roomed flat. But maybe you like the idea of an element per room in your house. Of course, the best thing would be to ask the spirits personally about your particular home, but my Teacher assures me that this basic idea will work in most places.

If you have just one room and wish to invite the elements in, then do so. But do it with intention. Open the windows and say:

'I invite the spirits of air into my home.'

Light a candle, or a fire in the grate, and say:

'I invite the spirits of fire into my home.'

Although an electric fire is still Fire, my spirits advise that it is good to consciously kindle a live flame in your life once a day.

Water can be in a vase, or a bowl to float flower heads and candles in. But it is easy to put these things in a room and then to forget about them until the flowers need changing. Once a day, run your hands under a tap and say,

'I invite the spirits of water into my home.'

Earth is often represented by crystals or by the compost in a pot plant. Again, it is easy to forget. Find a crystal or a stone that pleases you and find time, once a day, to pick it up and say:

'I invite the spirits of earth into my home.'

The elements are all around us, both in our environment and in ourselves. My Teacher gave me the following meditative, daily practice and you are welcome to try it if it appeals to you.

Stand or sit on the earth (preferably outside, but I know that this is not always possible). Have with you a candle, some matches or a lighter and a glass of water.

Feel the air all around you. Is it warm? Cold? Moving? Still? Now pay attention to your breath. Breathe in and out and be aware that the air that gives you life is the same air that moves the leaves on the trees. It is the same air that you and everyone else has breathed since the days we were all born. The air I breathe, you breathe. Say:

'The air is part of me. I am part of the air. We are one.'

Feel the earth beneath you. Is it concrete? Soil? Grass? Is it cold? Is it damp or dry? Be aware that all the creatures and all the plants on this planet are supported by the earth.

Now feel that earth inside you, in your bones and in your muscles. Say:

'The earth is part of me. I am part of the earth. We are one.'

Light the candle. If the air or the water is very enthusiastic today, your flame may go out as soon as you light it. Never mind. It is the intention behind the kindling of the flame that is important. You can always light a candle when you go indoors again. Be aware of the heat of the sun. Even if it is raining or foggy the sun is still there. We would not survive long if it were not. It is providing light and heat for everything on the earth – for everything in the solar system. Be aware of the heat around you and of the heat inside you. Say:

'The fire is part of me. I am part of the fire. We are one.'

Now drink the glass of water. Do it with intention. Feel the moisture in the air and in the earth. Now feel the moisture within yourself. Say:

'The water is part of me. I am part of the water. We are one.'

Sit for a while with all of the elements. Then thank the spirits and leave.

....

CHAPTER SEVEN

HAUNTING ISN'T ALWAYS DONE BY GHOSTS!

From the outside the house looked like any other mid-Victorian semi; three storeys, bay windows and faded gentility. A lovely family home in an English seaside town.

We knocked at the door and absorbed the atmosphere as we waited for our client to answer. She opened the stained-glass panelled door and ushered us inside to the front sitting room. There she told us why she had asked for the help of two shamanic practitioners.

Our client, Anne, had lived in the house for many years, at first with her two children and later alone. The house had never felt happy. There had been several deaths, including Anne's fourteen-year-old son. Eventually her daughter had left home, taking with her the family dog and declaring that, if she stayed, something dreadful would happen to her and to the dog.

So, for the past half dozen years, Anne had lived alone. She had tried letting the attic bedrooms to students but this had never felt comfortable. Over these years Anne had become interested in many 'New Age' practices, learning tarot, using crystals and visiting psychics. As her interest grew so did her sensitivity and she became aware that something shared her house.

She felt there had been a murder there. On the landing on the first floor, by the bathroom and toilet doors, she was frightened and uneasy. It seemed to her that a man in dark clothes had thrown a young woman down the stairs. Sometimes she felt that the woman, scarcely more than a child and dressed in blue, was watching her.

She had read that ghosts could be sent onwards by directing them to 'the light', but when she tried this it made no difference.

Worse was to come. She began to have nightmares. A huge, black animal was looming over her as she lay in bed, slavering on her from knife-like fangs. Anne was at her wits' end.

We had first met a few years previously when Anne, as part of her spiritual search, had attended a couple of shamanic workshops that Christine and I had given. Anne had decided that shamanism was not her path but then, out of the blue, she found our telephone number and, in desperation, called us to ask if we could help her.

Anne showed us around the house. It was shabby but clean and decorated with a great deal of love and care in pinks and greens. There were ornaments everywhere, together with crystals, different coloured candles and statues of Indian gods, Buddhas, Virgins and crucified Christs. Downstairs was clammy and the air was sticky. The top floor was light and airy. But the floor between was quite different from either. At the top of the stairs it was like stepping into an icebox. In one spot in particular there was a column of cold air. The atmosphere in the corridor was heavy and, despite the sunlight and the electricity, it seemed dim. We went into Anne's bedroom and were greeted with more religious statues. Anne's bed-head was against the wall next to the door, so that as she lay in bed with the door open she could see along the corridor to the top of the stairs. She explained that she had read a book on Feng Shui and that this had told her the best way to position her bed for a good night's sleep was with the head to the north.

We suggested that Anne settle herself downstairs with a magazine and a cup of tea, while we worked upstairs where the worst of the problem seemed to be. Then we went to the top of the stairs and discussed our strategy. Christine, as you know, works a lot with the spirits of the dead, helping those who are stuck or hurt to reach the Land of the Dead. At this point we were both assuming that ghosts were what we had to deal with, so we agreed that Christine would Journey first to sort out any souls that were still lingering in the house. She lay down and began to Journey to the spirit realms where her Spirit Teacher lives while I drummed.

When she came back she was a bit surprised. There had been no one stuck in the house. There was a little of what her Teacher calls 'dead stuff' – those bits of ourselves that we throw off when we are frightened, angry or deeply sad – and these Christine gathered and took to the Land of the Dead to be reunited with their owners, but of the ghosts we had expected there was no sign.

All buildings have spirits. The believer in shamanism knows that *everything* has a spirit. And we knew that any work we did in this house would have to include the house spirit. We decided that this was the time to visit the house spirit and to find out what was going on.

I Journeyed while Christine drummed.

At once my Teacher came and I asked him to introduce me to the house spirit. He grinned and beckoned me into the bedroom. There, in the middle of the room, was a spirit who appeared to be a girl in a blue, Victorian-style dress. She had long, straight blonde hair and a sulky expression. She also sported long fingernails and teeth, usually a sign of hostility. I asked her what was wrong.

'Everything! I don't want her in my house. She doesn't care about me. I want her to go!'

I pointed out that a house needs people to live in it and asked why she didn't want humans in the house.

She said, 'They've never taken any notice of me. They don't care about me. I'll kill them.'

She was seeing no difference between Anne and previous owners. 'They' were all bad. It is not normal for a house spirit to want to harm the people of the house – after all, houses are built to be lived in. But they can be hurt just as we can be and a hurt spirit, like a hurt human, will strike out at those nearby. Not always at those who did the hurting. And house spirits are like the rest of us – they like to have notice taken of them. This particular spirit was bitter and angry.

She told me, with some glee, that she had 'called in' – she made it sound like a tradesman – someone to help. And he had brought the 'Madra Dubh'. That would get rid of Anne.

I pointed out that if Anne died someone else would buy the house and come to live in it. She was lucky to have Anne, who had made an effort and would probably make more once she knew what was wanted.

My Teacher joined in and gradually she began to listen. She was not happy but we were determined and she finally acquiesced. I asked my Teacher about the Madra Dubh (which I could translate into 'Black Dog' only because there is an embroidery shop of that name which advertises in magazines I have read!). He said that we could get rid of that without much trouble now that we knew what it was. The problem might be with the man at the top of the stairs, the one who had brought the Madra Dubh. Since I was in the spirit realms I could see clearly the bolts of attacking energy that he was throwing off. They were bouncing down the stairs and were what Anne had thought was a body falling, and they were racing along the corridor, into Anne's bedroom and across the pillows of her bed. Across the place where her head rested at night. Anne's attempt at Feng Shui had unwittingly placed her in a very vulnerable position.

I asked my Teacher if the man was a demon.

He shrugged. 'You could call it that,' he said, enigmatically.

I stepped up to the 'demon' and asked him to leave. He laughed at me. Remember, he'd been told to 'go to the light' by Anne, not very long ago.

He said, 'Who do you think you are?'

I said, 'I'm a shaman.'

'Oh, shit!' he said.

Not that he gave up without a fight. Christine tells me I thrashed about in my Journey. Eventually my Teacher wrapped him in a golden rope and set off with him, and with the Madra Dubh.

'Where are you taking him?' I asked.

'Where he belongs,' he replied.

Then we went back to the house spirit. What could we do to make her happy? Not including, of course, getting rid of Anne.

She came back to the argument that no one took any notice of her. If we could ask Anne to acknowledge her, would that be all right? Maybe. She wanted a picture of her, in her blue dress, in the bedroom, with a candle or some flowers near it. She swept her hand around the room in disgust, taking in all the Buddhas, Shivas and Christs.

'All these and nothing of me!'

Okay, I could tell Anne that the picture was wanted.

'And I hate all this pink! Tell her to decorate in blue. And tell her all these foreign statues and Chinese bed-moving stuff doesn't work here.'

'I'll tell her,' I said, 'but I don't know that she'll listen.'

'No. Her mind's as cluttered as the house!'

I returned from my Journey and we went to tell Anne what had happened. I suggested gently that she should get rid of some of the clutter in the house.

'And try talking to the house spirit.'

'Oh, I do,' said Anne. I was surprised. Anne had thought the house spirit was a ghost but, even so, if she'd tried being friendly I didn't think the spirit would have been so bitter.

'What do you say?'

'I say, "I know you're there! Go away!"'

I had more in mind things like:

'Hello! I'm home from the shops.'

'I'm thinking of painting this room blue. Would you like that?' or

'Good morning.'

I hope Anne and her house spirit learn to get on. A house that has a happy house spirit is a friendly and contented home.

And most house spirits are friendly and happy. Houses are built to be lived in and most house spirits like a lived-in house. Anne's was an interesting case for many reasons. It was the first (although not the last) time that I had come across a demon. Or the notion that a discontented spirit might call in someone else to do her dirty work for her. This particular house spirit had been unhappy for a long time, since shortly after the house had been built. And, in this respect, house spirits, like land spirits, like other Middle World spirits, behave like humans. If they are hurt and embittered they will try to hurt others in return. That doesn't stop the vast majority of spirits, like the vast majority of humans, from being friendly and helpful.

We were asked to visit Alice's house, in Harrogate. Again, it was a mid-Victorian semi-detached house in a suburb. Alice was a young mother, at home all day with her two-year-old son, Ben. Her husband worked in Leeds and they had moved into the house only a few months previously.

Alice was scared. Things happened in the house. Pictures fell off walls and mugs smashed for no apparent reason. Alice would put Ben to bed, go downstairs and hear adult voices through the intercom. The kitchen in the house was in the basement and had a cellar leading off it, with a small window from the cellar onto the kitchen stairs. Alice would not go into the cellar. She felt that 'something's in there. Something horrible'. If she had to go into the kitchen she would rush in, do whatever she had to do and rush out again. She left most of the cooking to her husband who was aware of no presences in the house.

We were shown into the sunny front room and left alone while Alice went into the dreaded kitchen to make coffee. We compared first impressions. It was a beautiful house but it didn't feel lived in. It was more than not lived in, there was an emptiness that I found very disturbing. Alice came back, she told us about the things that happened in the house and then she showed us around. Downstairs, in the cellar, there was certainly a feeling of heaviness that wasn't pleasant. In the rest of the house was just the emptiness. We settled Alice in the sitting room while we went to assess the problem.

Upstairs the attic room had been made into a bedroom for Alice and her husband and that was the room in which we started. Christine began to rattle and gradually she sank into a trance state in which she could easily communicate with the spirits. And then the atmosphere changed. Something woke up.

This was why the house had seemed so empty. It wasn't that there was no house spirit but that the house spirit had been asleep until Christine's rattling had awoken him. Whatever was causing the problems it wasn't him. For a while he was rather confused, then curious. The house was still recognisably the same building that he had known a hundred years ago, when he had first gone to sleep, but many of the things inside had changed. So he had a tour of the house. The light switches were the first things he investigated.

'Oh! Ooh!' as the light went on, then off again. He was fascinated by the television and by Alice with her short hair and her

leggings. I think he was rather scandalised by the amount of ankle that she showed.

But it was the cuddly Tellytubby in Ben's bedroom that he liked the most. He pointed excitedly at the turquoise toy.

'Me. Me.' And indeed, although he did not have the same face nor, indeed, a television in his tummy, he was the same colour.

I asked him why he had gone to sleep.

'I was scared,' he said. 'It came in and I couldn't stop it. I couldn't get rid of it. So I hid upstairs and went to sleep.'

'It' turned out to be the entity in the cellar. We went down to have a look. As we passed the small window on the stairs something tried to grab me. I leapt back.

'It was a hand,' I said, rather shakily, to my Teacher.

'They're all talk and acting big,' he said with a confidence that I wished I could muster.

He helped me past the reaching hand, then turned to help the house spirit as well.

'That's it,' he said fearfully.

Inside the cellars it was dark, cold and damp. A hulking figure with long arms ending in clawed hands scowled at us.

'You don't belong here,' I said. 'Let us send you home.'

It shook its head.

'Staying here,' it said.

'But you are scaring the people who live here.'

'Good!'

I was prepared to go on arguing. My Teacher wasn't. He waved his hand and misty figures appeared behind us. They moved forward with a golden net, which they flung over the creature. Then they continued into the depths of the cellar and disappeared.

'Where have they taken it?' I asked.

'To where it belongs,' he said. I get the impression that he thinks I'm too soft some of the time.

'Has it gone for good?' the house spirit asked my Teacher.

He nodded. 'It won't come back now. You can get on with looking after this house and this family. You've a lot of time to make up.'

The house spirit looked a little sheepish and my Teacher smiled. He had sounded stern, but I think he was sympathetic.

'Look at this,' he said to the house spirit.

The house spirit looked where he pointed, at the dish of cat food. Then he looked up with shining eyes and a big hopeful smile.

'They've got a cat? A cat and a mummy and a daddy and a little boy! That's a real family!'

'And they need a real family home with a real family house spirit,' said my Teacher.

'Is there anything that Alice can do for you?' I asked.

The house spirit thought, then led me to the garden.

'I'd like a yellow flower planted, just there,' he said.

And the voices in Ben's room? I asked my Teacher who told me that they were Ben's spirit helpers, who came to tuck him in each night and keep him safe from the cellar inhabitant. Alice planted a yellow rose bush and redecorated the kitchen. It is now one of her favourite rooms.

In both Anne's and Alice's homes there was something in the house other than a house spirit. When we first moved into our present home there was only a very unhappy house spirit to contend with.

We moved into our house on 15 November 1995. It was in a dreadful state and for nearly three months we had no heating other than a small coal fire in the front room. But we knew it was the right place for us. After all, the spirits had led us here, every inch of the way. On the 17th the snow arrived. On the 18th some of our furniture arrived – a bed, a couple of chairs and a Baby Belling cooker. At least we could eat warm food. The rest of the furniture was in storage and arrived, courtesy of Pickfords, about a week later.

Having our bed meant that we could sleep upstairs in the bedroom, rather than in sleeping bags on the sitting-room floor. However, that is when I started having nightmares.

Christine was not sleeping well either, tossing and turning for half the night. I dreamed that something dark and fierce was chasing me through narrow, be-nighted streets. After a few nights like this we were worn out. I Journeyed to find out what was causing the problem.

My Teacher came to me and took me up to the bedroom. There she produced a rattle and rattled all around the bed. Something dark and goblin-like was sitting on the pillows. It seemed to be male, dark and wizened, with limbs long and thin like a spider's legs. And it seemed to be sitting in its own little black cloud.

I asked my Teacher who he was and she said he was something that I had to deal with. So I asked him. He glared at me. He said he was a boggle and it was his house, he hated us and he wanted us to go away.

'Why do you hate us?' I asked. 'You don't know us. We've only just moved in.'

'Don't care! All people are the same!'

Oh, dear.

The house was in a dreadful state. The last owners had used it as a holiday cottage, living in it for a couple of weeks each summer. It had not been maintained, looked after or loved. We were having several thousands of pounds' worth of work done on it.

'We care about this house,' I said. 'We chose it and we want it. We are dealing with the damp and the rot. We're going to have a range put in instead of the fire and back boiler in the kitchen. The house is going to be warm and dry.'

'And loved?' he asked.

'And loved,' I said.

Now the Boggle has a saucer of milk (or cream, if we're feeling rich) each evening. If we haven't had a fire in the sitting room we light a candle to honour the hearth as the heart of the home. If we are having work done to the house or we are decorating we let him know. If people are staying in the house we let him know. And if we are going away for a few days we warn him that there won't be a fire or milk for a while, but that soon we will come back. At first he was suspicious, expecting to be abandoned. Once he was so scared of being left that he pulled down a bookshelf. But he is happier now. He looks after us, we look after him and we both look after the house in our own ways. If he wants us to Journey to speak with him he signals by setting the mugs on their hooks swinging.

House spirits like different things. One asked for chocolate cake. Fresh flowers are a common request. And they seem united in their hatred of clutter. Several have wanted the house filled with 'nice smells' – potpourri, scented candles or oils.

The telephone call was from Janice and she was not happy.

'It's Jasper,' she said. Jasper was one of her cats. He'd developed a cancerous growth in his neck, which had been successfully removed. But the wound was not healing. Two weeks later it gaped, was inflamed around the edges and was oozing pus. He was a very sick cat. We made an arrangement to go round to see Jasper. Janice was a vet. If she could do no more for him, then the situation was serious.

When we arrived at the house, the following day, Janice was at work. Her partner, Judy, was on the telephone. She let us in and we discreetly moved into the sitting room. She was obviously in the middle of a row.

She finished her call and came into the sitting room to greet us. She was upset and angry. She and Janice had moved into this house only a few weeks before and she already hated it. Everything had been going wrong since they arrived. The phone call had been from Judy's ex-husband who was harassing her and laying claim to personal items of Judy's. Jasper was ill. On top of everything, she and Janice had started having violent arguments – totally out of character for both of them.

'It's really odd,' she said. 'We only fight when we're in the house. If we go out, we get on fine, just as we always did.' She went to get us coffee and Christine looked at me.

'It's heavy,' she said, referring to the atmosphere. Certainly the room was dull and lifeless. But then, it was an overcast day. Nevertheless, the things that Judy had told us sounded very much as if part of the problem, at least, was with the house.

Jasper was brought in, looking very sorry for himself. He had a huge dressing on his neck. His fur and eyes were dull. Even so, he was far from docile. Judy held him in her arms while we worked, for he wouldn't let us touch him.

Christine drummed. I Journeyed to meet my Healing Teacher.

She came to look at Jasper and shook her head slowly.

'He's not a well cat,' she said. She pointed out to me an intrusion in his neck, a small black creature that, as I was in a shamanic

state of consciousness, I could see clearly. She told me to rattle and sing over the creature, persuading it to come out of Jasper's neck. At first it was reluctant – it was happy and warm where it was. Then I sang to it of how my spirit helpers would take it home to where it belonged. And gradually it agreed to leave. Then my Teacher instructed me to put one hand on Jasper's head as I Journeyed to find him a power animal. He was not keen on this but she said a few words to him and he calmed down. I found him a canary and blew it into him. Judy put him back into his basket and, almost at once, he went to sleep.

I was uncomfortable about the state of the house and the fact that Judy and Janice were so unhappy there. Christine drummed while I Journeyed to see if I could speak to the house spirit.

He came at once. He was huge, brown, hulking and covered in fur. And he was cross and petulant.

'They don't care about the house. They didn't want to move here.'

Well, no, they hadn't.

I said, 'They can't be happy and want to be here if you are causing problems.'

'None of them cared. Look at the state it's in.' The house had been used for temporary accommodation for several years and was in need of some work doing to it. I agreed that the house spirit had a point. I said I'd tell Judy and Janice and ask them to do the repairs. He began to be mollified. Then he added, 'And it's so noisy with that kid crying all the time!'

I was surprised. Neither Judy nor Janice had children.

'What kid?'

'The boy in the front room. If you stop him crying, I'll stop causing problems.'

I went with my Teacher into the front room. In a corner was a small boy of about eight or nine. Judging from his clothes he was Victorian, which was another surprise. The house wasn't built until the 1970s. In the nineteenth century the area was marshland.

I approached him and said, 'Hello.'

He started in surprise. His face was dirty and tear-stained.

'Who are you?'

He didn't reply.

I tried again. 'What are you doing here?'

No, I clearly scared him too much for him to speak. I returned to Christine and Judy and told them what I had found.
Judy was fascinated by the description of the house spirit.

'It sounds like the Honey Monster!' she said.

Christine decided that she would ask her spirits about the boy, so I drummed and she Journeyed.

When she returned she told us what had happened. The boy was still afraid but Christine's Teacher spoke to him gently and elicited the information that his mother had told him to wait here until she returned. He was still waiting but, 'She's been a long time.'

About a hundred years, we think, although, as is common in such situations, he himself had no idea that it had been so long.

Christine and her Teacher took him and led him to where the Rainbow Bridge reaches up and into the Land of the Dead. There his mother was waiting for him, arms outstretched. They rushed to each other and embraced, the mother waved her thanks, they turned and walked over the bridge and Christine came back.

I went to tell the house spirit that the crying had stopped. He was sitting at the top of the stairs.

'Thank you,' he said, 'that kid was really getting on my nerves. He's been here all the time. I won't cause any more problems but tell her I like nice smells around the house.' And with that he waved his hand at me in dismissal.

I told Judy about the 'nice smells'. She has filled the house with scented candles and potpourri. When she cleans the stairs she finishes by spraying air-freshener around and says:

'Mind your eyes, Honey Monster!'

Her ex-husband got back in touch only once more – to say he was no longer interested in her things and was giving up his claims on them. And Jasper is well again and back to terrorising the local dogs.

David had recently moved into a small terraced house. He was one of our students and quite eager to meet the spirit of his new home so he set aside an evening to Journey and contact it.

He telephoned us.

'That was awful,' he said. 'I started by rattling around the house and suddenly the rattle just took off! It led me all over the house rattling madly. Then I started to Journey. The house was full of spirits. And the house spirit himself was really unfriendly.'

We went round the next evening. David had not slept well during the intervening night.

Christine Journeyed and, with the help of her Teachers, moved on the spirits of previous occupants of the house, now dead. Then, with our support, David went once again to speak to the house spirit. This time it consented to talk to, rather than shout at, David.

'How dare you grass over the garden,' he said. 'The garden is there to feed the family. How can the family eat grass?'

David tried to explain that he was the only person in the house. The house spirit found this unfathomable. Eventually David's spirit Teacher took over and gently explained to the house spirit that time had moved on. The small house, one of a terrace, was no longer inhabited by a miner or fisherman and his family. The mines were closed, the fishing fleet no longer existent. The garden was a place for relaxation, not food production. Gradually he accepted all this, although not gracefully. David promised that he would see what he could do about the garden, not being averse to fresh vegetables himself. Then another problem arose. The spirit of the garden joined in and he had ideas of his own.

'But I like roses in the garden!'

David reached a compromise. Half the tiny garden has flowers, including roses, and the other half is laid out as a vegetable patch.

Everything changes, everything has to grow. It isn't right for spirits to stick and stagnate any more than it is for humans to do so. And we have found that in homes that have continued to be used there is often no problem. Houses that have been empty for a long time often have spirits that are unhappy, for, after all, houses are meant to be lived in.

A death in a house doesn't often seem to disturb the house spirit. Death is part of life and, assuming that we are not talking here of a particularly horrific death – one, for example, preceded by torture – the house spirit does not seem to be worried. Even painful deaths are not a problem to the house spirit (although they might be to the deceased or to his or her family) so long as they are not deliberately brought about.

Near our home is a ruined terrace of cottages, uninhabited since the depression finally destroyed the industry in Rosedale. They saw many deaths during the years they were inhabited and there is an air of sadness about them. Periodically we go up there to do some more work to settle the unhappy spirits. But this is because these houses have not been lived in since these deaths happened. The deaths were an ending, not part of the cycle of life. The sadness of a young mother losing her three children on one day has seeped into the stones for there has been no happiness since to replace the sorrow.

An empty house is no longer able to do what it was made to do and it becomes stuck. It cannot move on or develop. If, after several years, it is again inhabited, it may well resent the fact that its new owners do not act in the same way as the old ones that it is still remembering. This is what we think had happened with David's house spirit. He knew where he was with the old miners who grew cabbages and carrots in the garden.

Even worse for the spirit is when, after a period of emptiness, the building changes use.

The old mill in the Lancashire town had been standing empty for years. Now it had been divided into units and was being sold piece-meal. One of the units had been bought by our client, Sylvia, who was using her unit to run a small organic food shop. She felt that the place was haunted, having become aware of the old man who looked over her shoulder whenever she was sitting at her computer in a corner of the storeroom. Not that she minded. She felt that he was a benign presence. She was more concerned in case he had some sort of message for her and, having no way of contacting him herself, other than simply talking to him which had elicited no response, she wanted us to do it for her. Christine and I arrived on a rainy Lancashire day after a long and wet drive over the Pennines. Following Sylvia's directions, we eventually found the mill and parked. The whole area was in transition, with parts looking very run-down, others relatively smart and the rest resembling a builders' site. Sylvia's shop was small and dusty, with a very cluttered storeroom at the back. The skylights were grimy and cracked and the toilet and wash area were dirty. Sylvia clearly had very little money with which to 'do up' the shop.

Christine and I set up a working area, cleaning it as best we could and making a small altar with candle, incense, water and a small piece of brick. Whenever we make an altar we try to include a local stone so that our work is anchored in the land. In this case there were no stones around, so we used the piece of brick made from local clay. It's still from the land.

Then I drummed and Christine rattled her way around the shop before Journeying to find any souls that might have become stuck there over the years. As there had been in Anne's home there was very little 'dead stuff'. We didn't think that the problem was one of a ghost. Christine drummed and I Journeyed. Almost at once I contacted the old man. As we thought, we were not dealing with a ghost but with the mill spirit. He was annoyed and grumpy.

'Look at the mess! Vegetables all over. And what's that?' he said in a scornful voice, pointing at the notice over the door. 'Org-ann-iks. What's that supposed to mean?'

I explained what organic meant. He was horrified.

'How else can you grow vegetables?'

Somewhat mollified he admitted that maybe this was a good use of the space. I spoke to him for a long time of how things moved on and changed. How the mill could no longer be used as a mill because the world had changed and cotton was not being brought to the town to be processed as it once was. Of course, the mill spirit had no wider view of the world. The fact that his mill, which had produced cloth and was useful, was now being used for vegetables seemed to him to be the whim of a few humans rather than related to the economics and politics of world trade.

Eventually my Teacher put it to him as an opportunity for him to have new experiences and to develop as a spirit. He looked around.

'All right. If they mend the windows and clean up in here.'

Mending windows takes money but I could see what he meant about the clearing up. I returned to tell Sylvia that, if she would keep the place more tidy and promise to mend the windows when she could afford it, the mill spirit was prepared to lend his influence to making the shop a success.

Sometimes, with all our efforts, we cannot negotiate with a spirit. Mandy had asked us to help because she was having a lot of problems. She heard voices when she was alone in the house, one area of the sitting room was cold and very unpleasant to stand in and Mandy was afraid to be alone at night.

The flat was one of several, converted from an old Methodist chapel. Mandy was a 'New Age' pagan. When I first made contact with the spirit of the chapel I was confronted by a very angry spirit.

'She's a wicked woman and has no place in a holy building!'

I tried to point out to him that time had moved on. The chapel had been converted into flats because fewer people visited the chapel each Sunday and people needed homes in which to live. He was unconvinced. From his point of view his entire purpose was to look after the chapel in which Methodists came to pray each week. This purpose had been taken away from him. He resented that he was no longer a chapel and was bitterly angry that such a person as Mandy had moved in. He was determined to get rid of her, even more than all the other people who lived in the flats. I turned to my Teacher for help.

'There's nothing that you can do,' he said. 'If there were any chance of getting the co-operation of everyone in the flats then, maybe, we could sort something out. The situation needs a community ritual. But there isn't any chance of that.'

I returned from my Journey and advised Mandy to move home as soon as possible.

We were asked to help a man who owned a dry-cleaners in a small Yorkshire town. His machines had been breaking down and one had boiled at the wrong time, ruining a customer's suit. The manufacturers had replaced the machine but to no avail. Things were still going wrong. He was mid-European and sure that someone had put the evil eye on his business, since that possibility was part of his culture.

I was prepared to believe that someone could be working ill against him but, in my experience, this is rare. I Journeyed to find out what was happening. Not greatly to my surprise I discovered that the shop spirit was causing the problems.

'I hate him with his big, noisy machines! They're ugly! I'm going to break them all!' She was not amenable to reason. The shop had, until recently, been a gift shop. She had liked that. The place had been full of pretty ornaments, scented candles and wind chimes. There had been tinkly New Age music and – 'pretty things. Not like these ugly, noisy things!'

I've heard it said that there is no wisdom to be found in the Middle World. I disagree. I've found help, wisdom and great compassion from the spirits of many things that I have contacted in the Middle World. But, every now and again I come across a spirit who seems determined to change my mind about this. The shop spirit did not impress me with either her wisdom or her intelligence.

'I'm breaking his machine. Look.' She pointed proudly at the machine and I could see that tiny black spears stuck out wherever there was a join in a pipe and from behind the thermostat.

'Elf shot,' my Teacher explained. I was intrigued. I had read about elf shot but had never come across it before.

'What should I do about it?' I asked.

'It's easy to get out. You can use your rattle. But she'll just put it back unless you can persuade her not to.'

'Me?' He is much more persuasive than I am.

He grinned and waved me forward.

I took the spirit on a tour of the shop.

'Look at all these pretty things,' I said. Someone had brought in a military uniform to be cleaned and I showed her the braiding on the shoulders and the embroidery of the regimental badge. I found an evening dress of green silk and a blouse covered in flowers. I pointed out that there were many gift shops in this town but only one dry-cleaners. It was special. The only shop that was dedicated to keeping the people of the town clean (I kept my thoughts carefully away from the chemist's and the hairdresser's). And all the time I was thinking, 'She'll never fall for this …'

But she did, gradually.

'I'll have to be clean as well,' she said, musingly. 'If he'll have fresh flowers on the counter and put me out a bowl of water every Saturday night after the shops closed, so I can wash, I'll not break the machines. And I'll look after the shop as well.'

So not only houses have spirits. As we have seen, shops have them as well. Our friend, Monica, who lives in a caravan, has caravan spirits. Like the spirit in the dry-cleaner's they like fresh water and flowers. They certainly didn't like the caravan being moved to a new site without them being told.

'You packed all your cups and glasses safely away, but you didn't even warn us that our home was going to be moved. We were thrown all over the place! You didn't care about that, did you?'

Monica apologised and the spirits were mollified. Since then she says that the caravan has been 'more homely'. A bowl of water, some fresh flowers, a drink of milk or even the occasional slice of cake seems a small price to pay for a happy home.

People often ask me how to go about 'cleansing' their house. I must emphasise that this will not solve problems with an angry house spirit, or a seriously disturbed ghost. If you have something that you cannot deal with, get in a professional. But if you just want to 'psychically freshen up' your home, or clear the air after an argument, or create a special space for spiritual work, then, please, try these ideas. Use incense, in cones, sticks or 'smudge'. Sprinkle salt – although this does involve getting out the sweeper afterwards. Sprinkle water or use a rattle. Whatever you use, remember that it is your intention to clear the space of any energies that are not helpful to you. Your intention is the important thing here.

Probably the most significant thing that you can do to encourage a happy home is to make a friend of your house spirit. I have said already that we give ours a saucer of milk each evening. Maybe you would feel a little silly doing this if you haven't actually met the house spirit. But you can still honour your home.

Where is the centre of your home? Is it the kitchen stove? The fireplace? In times gone past the hearth would have been the centre of the home and would have been honoured accordingly. Now, in these days of central heating, not all houses have a hearth. You must decide for yourself where the home's centre is. It might be the table around which the family gathers for a meal or the worktop where you prepare your family's food. I suggest that you don't choose the television set, even though this is often where the family gathers together. This is not because of any disapproval of television but because the heart of the home should be a place to focus on the home. Television takes us out of the home and into the wider world. This is good for our connection to the world but not good for honouring our home and its spirits.

When you have decided on the centre, make a small shrine. This does not have to be obvious. Again, it is your intention that is important. We have a candle or flowers on our dining table and, on nights when the fire isn't lit, we light a candle in the grate.

And talk to your house spirit. Even if you can't hear the reply, your friendly voice will help. Explain any changes that are to be made to your house, whether it is a new sofa or a loft conversion. Tell your house spirit when you have friends staying or if one of the family will be away from home overnight. And if you move house, thank the spirit of your old house for taking care of you, and, when you arrive in your new home, introduce yourself.

CHAPTER EIGHT

WORKING WITH SPIRITS OF THE LAND

I hadn't been working with the spirits long before I was asked to do a soul retrieval. It was for an oak tree with whom I'd been working and, although at the time I didn't have a clue what to do, my spirits were keen to get me started on this. They showed me how to do it, I did the work, and a week later the tree had put out new leaves, something that oaks often do in summer, but unlike the other oaks around this one had not been doing so. It was a wonderful thing to have done but, at the time, I thought very little of it in terms of doing more of the same. In the next few years I did a soul retrieval for my garden and one for a beech tree in Sherwood Forest, but little else.

Then, some time after this first soul retrieval, I did a Journey to talk to the spirits. I asked, 'What is my part of the contract with the spirits?', and I was told, among other things, to heal the land. How was I to do this? They said, 'We'll tell you when you need to know!'

A year later I was in Devon, attending a shamanic workshop. We were sent out to find a power place. 'Nearby' were the teacher's words. I ended up about a mile and a half away but there was no denying that this was the right place. I'd never before felt a signal from the spirits so strongly. The summer was hot and the horseflies were out in strength. My power place was under trees beside the stream.

Our Journey was to ask the spirits of the power place for help during the week's work. I'd done things like this before and was expecting it to be straightforward. The first lesson that I learned on this Journey was 'Don't be complacent'.

I found myself surrounded by a crowd of spirits, of all shapes and sizes. They all seemed very suspicious. What did I want?

I explained that I needed their help to do some healing work. They seemed doubtful. Why should they help me? What was in it for them? One of my personal helpers got a bit irritated by this and pointed out that if I learned healing it would benefit everyone. They agreed but were not mollified. I asked if I could do anything for them in return. They didn't think so, but my spirit helper sniffed around and reported that, 'The Stream has lost its soul.'

The spirit of the place who seemed to be doing the most talking looked at me. I looked at him. Then he said, grudgingly, 'If you'll help our Stream, we'll help you.'

There followed a real adventure which, I must admit, I enjoyed thoroughly, with much dashing and daring, captured maidens and fierce monsters. The Stream had been kidnapped by the River King. My helpers and I rescued her. When we returned to the power place there was much hugging and kissing of the Stream from the other spirits of the place. Eventually they remembered we were there and turned to me. Yes, they said. The Stream would help me this week in return for what I'd done for her.

And for a while she did. For the next two Journeys, when I was healing, she came and helped. Then I made a mistake. I took Christine to see the power place. We realised at once that the spirits did not want her there, for the horseflies, which had held off me until then, began to bite in earnest.

The next time I called for her the Stream didn't come.

I Journeyed to the place again.

They didn't want to let me in. I insisted that they listen to me. I apologised for taking Christine there but they were still not happy. Finally, I left and, as I turned to go, the Stream spirit suddenly scratched my face. My helpers pushed her away and pulled me back.

My Teacher said, 'Don't go there again.'

The next day the ash tree near the workroom spoke to me. It explained that the land had been hurt by many humans and that the

River King is the anger of the land. He is particularly angry about the ways the moors are being treated.

'The moors are the heart of this land and the humans use them for war and imprisonment.'

It is not difficult to see that this must have an effect on the spiritual health of the area and, therefore, on the attitudes of the spirits of the area, but the land is not treated any better in many other places. I'd never had such a hard time from the spirits anywhere else. The ash tree replied:

'In the north, in your home, the land knows you. Here you are just another human, out to take and not give.'

Now, I wasn't having a particularly easy time in my personal life just then and maybe if that hadn't been so I wouldn't have been so affected by the depth of feeling I had received from the land there in Devon. And maybe I wouldn't have needed the healing a month or so later to fetch back the piece of soul that the Stream had snatched in that last scratch. Certainly there were a lot of lessons to be learned from the incident and a lot of thinking about it to be done.

I know that it can be an unpopular and uncomfortable notion that the spirits are anything other than constantly supportive and loving towards us. It can be hard to accept that the spirits may have feelings, emotions and motivations that have nothing to do with us. We grant this capacity to other humans, most of the time, but often that is as far as we are at ease with. I missed something important about what was going on in Devon. Something that I picked up on instantly the next time it happened.

I've spent fifteen years teaching children with special needs. Sometimes this has been with children who have specific learning difficulties or specific physical difficulties only. This is rare. More often the learning problems are inextricably entangled with behavioural problems. I once taught for a memorable while in a hospital unit for children who were psychiatrically disturbed, often as a result of horrific abuse. What I became very aware of with those children is hate. It comes off them in waves. To begin with it was very hard to cope with but the hate wasn't directed personally at me. I began to see it as self-hate that spilled out onto anyone else who was around. When someone is in that state all they can do is hit out. I began to interpret the hate as pain, as an inarticulate plea for help. Or as an attempt to get me to hate them so much I'd just leave them alone in their misery.

Very shortly after we moved to the North Yorkshire Moors, in November of 1995, I began to have a series of clumsy accidents – falling on the ice and such like. I'm not usually that careless. I asked my spirits about this. They said:

'Part of the valley doesn't want you here. If you hurt yourself, if you break a leg, you'll have to go to hospital and you'll be out of the valley.'

'Why does part of the valley want me to go?' I asked.

'You'll find out soon,' they told me.

Six days after that Journey we went for a walk over the other side of the valley. Suddenly our dog, Cafell, stopped. There was a section of path along which she would not walk. Nor would she walk on the moor to either side of it. Christine had her rattle with her and began to move around the area, dancing and singing, seeking for the source of the problem. As I sat and watched her, letting the rattle change my consciousness, I became aware of a darkness and a heaviness over that part of the moor, not only on the surface but also deep inside the earth.

Watching Christine rattle, or drum, when she is working is an incredible experience. She sings, chants, dances and the power is tangible. When she had finished Cafell trotted forward quite happily along the path, pausing only to give us one of her 'Come on, what are you waiting for?' looks.

That night I Journeyed about this. I was told:

'It lives here, the thing that doesn't want you in the valley. You're attracting its attention.'

My curiosity was aroused. So was my compassion. I recognised this attitude. In many ways I was ready for it as I had not been in Devon. The land was saying, 'Go away and leave me alone!'

I had a lot to do before my spirits were satisfied that I was ready to help that part of the moor. There was a shirt to decorate with ribbons and a staff and a necklace of bones to make. Then I needed a spirit who would agree to help me with this work. My spirits led me to a place on the moor where I found a horse's skull. I took it home and, under their direction, cleaned it and decorated it with ribbons. Then I Journeyed to its spirit, a skeletal horse, to ask if it would help me. It was happy to do so.

Rosedale has been industrial for centuries. There has been jet mining and glass-making here since at least the twelfth century. But it was in 1856 that the extraction of the highest-grade ironstone in Europe began, to feed the steel mills of Teesside. Rosedale was transformed as three pits were opened and a railway was constructed to take the ore over the moors to Middlesbrough. By 1930 it was all over and now the valley has just the ruins of lime kilns left, a few rows of Victorian cottages which were built for the workers and the route of the railway, now a footpath, around Rosedale, over to Farndale and on to join the Esk Valley line at Battersby.

I was told that the moor needs the spirits that were dragged away with the ironstone to be brought back to it. It has been grieving for over a hundred years. My Teacher told me that I was to walk around the route of the railway until it left the moors, 'and you'll know where that is', as a lament for the lost spirits. I was to chant and sprinkle seawater the entire way while dancing with my staff. When I reached the edge of the moors I was to sing back the spirits that had been lost.

I set off at about ten o'clock on a spring morning. The first few miles were simple. I thought about what I was going to do but I knew that I hadn't really started yet. I wore my shirt decorated with ribbons and was glad there were not many other people out to see me. Suddenly I reached a gateway, as clear as if its stones had been in Ordinary Reality. I took a breath and stepped through. What I experienced was:

'I am the moor. It is me. We are. I was taken from the moor when I was first fashioned. My bones are gritstone and sandstone. My blood vessels are limestone with the clear, sweet mountain water flowing through them. The plants with their tenacious roots are my sinews and the soil clothes my bones with muscles. The creatures of the moor are the nerve impulses, carrying their messages to and fro.'

I sang a song that my spirits sang through me as I made my way along the route. Sometimes it was a dirge, sometimes it was a song of encouragement for the spirits, sometimes it was clearing a way for their return. Often it was a low growl, occasionally a shout. And always I was in three states of mind. Part of me was in Ordinary Reality, checking the route, watching where I was putting my feet. Part was a hundred years ago, with the trucks of iron ore on the Victorian railway, rattling their way north. Most of me was with the spirits of that ore and that was like walking beside cattle trucks bound for Dachau. Silent, wide-eyed spirits were clasping the sides of the trucks, and each other.

When I reached the top of Ingleby Incline it was hard to believe that the trucks had ever been up and down it. In a kilometre the land drops 340 metres. I knew that steel ropes had been used to haul the wagons up and down and I expected a slow, steady descent.

What actually happened was that the place went crazy. The trucks careered over the edge and accelerated down the Incline with spirits screaming in terror and my spirit helpers doing their best to hold them back. I sang and stamped. Then, two-thirds of the way down, I came to another gateway, as tangible as the first. I stopped in front of it and, as instructed, I faced the distant Teesside and sang the spirits of the moor back home. I had a last sight of them rushing past me then I stepped through the gateway and was fully back in Ordinary Reality. I washed my hands in the last of the seawater then walked down the path and along the road to the point at which I'd arranged to be collected, about eighteen miles from where I had started.

That night I Journeyed.

> *I rode my horse of bones over the moors to Ingleby Incline, and sang and danced. The spirits came, in a huge rush, all shapes and sizes, hanging on to the ribbons of the horse's tail. We rode back over the route I'd walked, past the head of Farndale and over the ridge to Rosedale.*

Next day Christine drove me to the top of the ridge and I danced the spirits into the moor. The entire experience had been so intense that I felt it was exactly what I had been born to do. It was several days before I could find anything else of importance.

A few days later I saw a picture in a book belonging to a neighbour. It was an old photograph of trucks in a heap at the bottom of Ingleby

Incline. Apparently large numbers of the descents finished in crashes as the workers lost control. There were some dreadful accidents.

Healing the land is a large part of my shamanic work. I find that it isn't always understood. I come across people who have a happy little fantasy that although we've messed up the cities, the countryside, 'out in nature', is inviolate. It can be easy to see that the cities need healing, but not so easy to see that what we think of as 'country' may well need it too. Apart from the tops of some of the highest Scottish mountains there are no parts of the British Isles that are not human-formed. It may be easier to ignore the work of humans on a moor or in a forest than it is in the middle of a city, but the moor and forest are no less artificial landscapes, and often no less in need of healing.

This dichotomy of 'city' and 'country' can cause us to miss the opportunities to do shamanic work in those areas that are not thought of as so 'spiritual' or 'sacred'. I went to ask my Teacher why some places in the landscape are perceived as sacred, while others are not.

My Teacher said, 'There are energies that flow through all things, including humans. Sometimes a human's energy resonates with the earth's energy in a particular place. Then you'll find a place that's good for you to work with. Different people find different places, usually. These are personal power places. But, as you know from your own experience, a group of people who work together can often be drawn to the same place. If enough of you feel "right" there then it's a good place for group work. All places are sacred. If people look for a site for something in particular – healing, for example – they will find sites whose energies resonate with that issue.

There are practical considerations, of course. Stonehenge had to be built on a place large enough to get it all in. Castlerigg had to fit onto a flat, high place within the existing stone circle of the mountains.

'If you choose a place and work with it for long enough with enough intention then the energies will change to make it a more powerful site. This is what happens in your garden. It is what happened with Peter Foster's new stone circle at Lime Tree Farm. Places have different energies but all places are sacred.'

I asked, 'So why are some seen as more sacred than others?'
He said, 'Because it makes people feel safe and happy to do so.'

Recently our local Drumming Group all Journeyed on this same question. These are some of the answers that were given.

'All places are sacred. Stonehenge is perceived as such but all places should be honoured.'
'All places are sacred, holy.'
'Ancient sites are chosen by where they are in the landscape. They are seen as sacred because that is how they are perceived.'
'The most sacred place is always in your own heart.'
'People make places sacred by contacting spirits there.'
'All and no places are sacred.'
'Our power places are the places where the spirits called out to us.'
'Spirit talkers and shamans choose places just as we do. Sometimes they simply introduce their apprentices to their own places instead of sending them out to find their own. This way, some places come to be seen as sacred by a whole community. When you are healing the earth be careful. Places are in balance with other places.'
'Sacredness is a human perception.'

I also asked my Teacher, 'What is the spiritual distinction between country and urban landscapes?'

He said, 'There isn't one. People think there's a difference but people will think all kinds of things. Have you ever seen any difference between the spirits in a city and those in the country, more than the differences that you see in any two spirits anywhere?'
I said that I hadn't.
He went on, 'In any case, "urban" and "rural" are to do with perceptions. Geographically, Pickering [our nearest town] is urban but many of the people who live there call it "the country".'

A year or so after I had done the work for Rosedale Moor something happened that led to further work for the valley. We found that we were very tired. A few full nights' sleep were not shifting it.

Three neighbours, in the space of a week, mentioned to me how low they were feeling. Christine reported the same from the people that she spoke to. I went to find out what was happening.

As soon as Christine started drumming the room was full of clamouring, shouting spirits. I shouted to my Teacher and she quietened them.

I said, 'I want to help but you'll have to tell me or show me what is wrong.'

They took me to the River Seven, which flows through the valley. It was murky and sluggish. I asked my Teacher what was wrong with it. She said that it was ill and its energies were blocked.

'You should go, with Christine and Cafell if they are willing to help, to the source on the river, up on the moor. Then, staying as close as you can to the water, in it if possible, go downstream. Go under bridges rather than over them. At each bridge, confluence or deep pool give the spirit of that place a gift. Continue down the river to the confluence with Hartoft Beck. Each time you give a gift, rattle and say:

"'Greetings, Spirit. I am ... [giving my spirit name]. *I bring you a gift in token of the good work that you do."*

'Take your staff and your rattle.'

I asked what would be a suitable gift and was told that the spirits wanted the decorative glass nuggets that were in a bowl in our sitting room.

I don't know why river spirits should seem to want decorative but otherwise, seemingly, useless things like glass nuggets. Maybe they value decoration, maybe they have a use for them that has not occurred to me or maybe they just wanted a gift. I was delighted to oblige, whatever the reason.

And so, the following week, I did as I was requested. Christine was happy to help and Cafell was keen on any activity that promised a long walk. The walk took several hours and, by the end of it we were tired, cold, muddy and wet. We were able to stick to the river most of the way. The route through the village itself had to be on the road, although in sight of the river, and at one point we were so far from the river that we had to

throw a blue nugget into the tributary stream and hope that it
would be near enough.

I Journeyed again.

*The river was clear and sparkling. As my Teacher took me in
Non-ordinary Reality the route that we had followed in
Ordinary Reality I could see the spirits waving and laughing. I told
her that I was anxious about the blue nugget that I'd had to throw into
the stream. She took me to the place. There was the spirit of that confluence, a thin, spindly, grey figure. In his hands, held carefully, was the
blue, glass nugget. I told him that I had been worried he wouldn't get
it and he laughed.*

*'I climbed up the stream. It was waiting for me. Would you like to
see where I'm going to put it?'*

I said that I would, very much, and he led me beneath the water.

*I found myself in a small and cosy room, dimly lit by a gas lamp.
What little floor space existed was filled with armchairs and side tables.
One of these tables was circular and covered with a dark red cloth. The
spirit pulled this into the centre of the room. Then he knelt and, rever-
ently, placed the glass nugget in the middle of the table.*

'Thank you so much,' he said, quietly.

Christine also took a Journey to the valley. She said, 'The spirit of
Rosedale was an enormous, rainbow-coloured dragon. It was dancing its way down the river.'

One of our neighbours, who had known about our walk,
commented a day or so later, 'I don't understand all this stuff you
do but, whatever it was, it's worked. Everything seems so much
brighter and more positive, somehow.'

The following month Christine and I were walking Cafell along
the road in Rosedale when we became aware of a huge, black cloud
over our heads. Not that black clouds in Rosedale are rare but this
time the rest of the sky was a clear blue. Once again, when I got
back to the house, I went to consult my Teacher.

*I rose up slowly to the black cloud and asked if I might see its
spirit. The cloud turned into a huge black dragon. I asked the*

dragon what it wanted and it said that it was the spirit of Eskdale [the next valley to the north] *and had come into Rosedale because it had felt the changes in the energy.*

'We haven't anyone to do this sort of work in Eskdale,' he said. 'I came to see if help could be obtained.' He was very polite. I looked at my Teacher.

She said, 'Do you want to help?'

'Yes,' I said.

'Then between May and the end of July we will work in Eskdale,' she said. 'Until then, Rosedale needs our work.' It was then late February.

The Dragon bowed.

'It is good,' he said, and left.

And so, in May, I went to find out what work was to be done in Eskdale. The first piece of work that was required was to clear blockages in the River Esk. I was somewhat relieved that I did not have to do this in the same way as we had to for the River Seven. The Esk is a great deal longer! I had to find the bridge that curves like the top of an egg and rattle there. The blockage was beneath this bridge. The black dragon, looking sick and fed up, showed me the bridge in Non-ordinary Reality. I did not know Eskdale well. I drove down the valley hoping that I would recognise the bridge. And of course, I did. It looked exactly as it had done in my Journey. It is an old, narrow bridge and the road crosses the river at a ford beside it. I parked and went down to the river for a closer look.

'Stand in the water,' said my Teacher, as I started rattling in order to shift my awareness. I did so.

The water was cold. Directly under the bridge it felt greasy and most unpleasant.

'The blockage is under the water,' my Teacher said. 'Rattle under the water.'

'My rattle is made of rawhide,' I pointed out. 'It'll go soggy!'

'Nevertheless, that's the only way to do it,' she said.

139

And so I stood, for about half an hour, calf-deep in the River Esk, first rattling over my head and then leaning over and bringing the rattle down, into the water and through my legs. Then standing up and beginning again, over and over. By the time my Teacher said, 'It's done,' and I stopped, three cars had been parked by the road so that their drivers and passengers could watch this strange woman rattling in the water.

My poor rattle survived the experience but has a distinct wobble in it now!

I have found that it is not unusual for large areas of land, like a valley, to have dragons as their spirits. The next valley to the west of Rosedale, Farndale, has a green dragon and the Vale of Pickering has a bronze dragon.

In 1997 my sister asked me to visit her in Hong Kong where she has lived for many years. As well as a family holiday, my spirits told me, this was to be work. I was flying out in the middle of June and would return in early September. During that time Hong Kong would cease to be a British colony and would become, once more, part of China. Both Hong Kong and China were very different from what they had been like when last they were one country. The spirits of Hong Kong, I was told, would be uncertain and apprehensive. I spoke to the Teacher who helps me when I am in China. Although I can, and do, speak to my main Teacher in China, and my Chinese Teacher in England, I find that the perspective of a spirit who knows China well and who has lived there in several incarnations before he became a spirit Teacher is helpful when dealing with Chinese spirits.

'Poor Hong Kong,' my Teacher said, shaking his head. 'Poor China.' Then he shrugged.

'They're not the only places that are suffering. We can only do what we can do. The spirits there need to know that they are wanted, that the Reunification is happening because China wants them, not because the UK doesn't. The candle lit in Hong Kong will illuminate China.'

They were not the only spirits who were uncertain and apprehensive. Our house spirit in Rosedale was also very frightened that I wouldn't come back. I was left in no doubt of this when he pulled a shelf off the wall in the sitting room.

> *I explained that I would come back in a couple of months. He looked to my Teacher for confirmation. She agreed.*
> *'But one day you'll go away for good.'*
> *My Teacher said, 'When she does you can go with her.' She pointed to the shelf and looked at him. She was trying to look stern but there was a twinkle in her eye. The Boggle looked defiant.*
> *'I didn't want her to go away.'*

My first task in Hong Kong was to Journey to meet the spirits there. There were hundreds! My Teacher conveyed to me their thanks for coming then said to them:

'She will be setting up a clinic after next week. Remember, she's English. She'll like an orderly queue.'

I had a week to relax, then the spirits queued up to see me. There was something very Chinese about the idea of a clinic for the spirits, befitting a place that has possibly the most bureaucratic heaven in the world, and spirits take examinations in order to become gods. The first in the queue was the Peak Fountain. It wanted some lemon juice put into its water. This seemed a strange request and I asked why. I was told that a murder had been committed there some years ago. Armed men had attacked another man. In Non-ordinary Reality the blood was still there. The lemon juice would wash it away.

This was followed by a soul retrieval for a block of flats. Then the rattling of a pool of stagnant water in a park. In Non-ordinary Reality the water changed into butterflies.

I did an extraction for an area of the Peak, and freed some energy that showed itself to me as a baby dragon, from Garden Road. There were many things to do during late June and early July, before Reunification. One more was for the Peak Fountain.

> *My Teacher took me up to the Peak and laid me down on the fountain, in the water. This was very nice. The cool water splashed all over me. Then my Teacher suggested that I go down one*

*of the holes out of which the water comes. I tried and couldn't. They
were blocked.*

My Teacher said, 'Hong Kong is blocked from its spirit realms.'

*I tried to clear the holes from above but this was not possible so we
found a pipe that took us down, below the fountain, and tried to
unblock it from below. Mud and general gunge came out of the holes
and my Teacher gathered it up to take away.*

*He said, 'There'll be more work to do in the future and other trips
to Hong Kong.'*

*I felt overwhelmed by the thought of trying to administer to the whole
of Hong Kong. There must be other people here who can do this work.*

He smiled. 'When you come again you will teach some of them.'

The Reunification came and went and I was told by my spirits and
the spirits of Hong Kong that I'd done a good job. On the last
Journey I did to help Hong Kong, during that stay, my Teacher
looked really happy. He was dressed in blue and gold robes and
wore a tasselled hat.

*He took me to the top of the Peak and told me to look down on
how wonderful Hong Kong was.*

'You've helped get Hong Kong through a bad time,' he said.

*He sat me down, gave me black tea and told me to rest. I asked
what he was going to do.*

'I'm going to dance the night away,' he said.

The following spring Christine went to Hong Kong, among other
reasons, to help my sister move from one flat to another, nearby. My
sister was unhappy. The electrics in the flat she was moving from were
playing up, the washing machine kept flooding and there were ants
and cockroaches everywhere. These are a fact of life in the Tropics
but this was a real infestation! Christine's first piece of work was to
contact the spirits of the old flat, which was due for demolition.

She wrote:

I began by rattling in my spirits in the kitchen. Almost immediately,
I felt a dreadfully powerful feeling of grief and an overwhelming

loneliness welling through me. I began crying and wailing. This continued through the rooms of the flat, worst by far in the kitchen and bathroom but also bad in two of the bedrooms. The rattling slowed and was lethargic, hopeless, and the wailing became more and more desolate. I was crying as I sorted out the tape machine in order to visit the spirits of the flat in Non-ordinary Reality.

I found myself confronted by an angry Chinese official, demanding things loudly and incomprehensibly in Cantonese. A small, slight man in a blue robe stood to my left and replied to the angry official mildly, also in Cantonese. The official huffed and puffed but grudgingly accepted whatever he had been told.

I asked the man in blue who he was. He bowed to me and told me his name. He said that he would introduce me to the spirits of Hong Kong who could help me or who needed help.

'The spirits of this block are very distressed,' he said. 'The accumulated griefs of half a century are in them. They have not been honoured for most of this time and they are confused and bewildered with all the change around them. No one has explained it to them and they are frightened.'

I asked how I could help.

He shrugged. 'Almost you have come too late. This is the first family to be leaving this block. Many others will do so over the next months and you can do nothing for them. For the spirits of this flat you can do little. On the day of the move, when all the furniture has been taken, when all the people have gone, then make some tea and sprinkle it around the flat. Light some incense and offer it to the spirits of the block as a thank-you and as a humble acknowledgement of all they have done.'

But first there was the new flat to be cleaned, both physically and spiritually. Christine rattled around the flat and then Journeyed to her new Chinese Teacher who introduced her to the spirit of the place.

Then we walked around the flat. On the wall of the sitting room he wrote a character, which he translated as 'harmony'. In the office he wrote characters for 'diligence' and 'prosperity'. Elsewhere in the flat were written 'calm', 'love', 'joy'. By the front door was 'safety' and 'protection'. Each character, as he wrote it, glowed golden for a moment, then faded into the wall.

In February of 2000 we were back in Hong Kong. We were again visiting family and also giving some workshops in shamanism as my Teacher had told me I would. And of course, there was more work there to help the land.

Christine asked her spirits about this.

I went to Stanley, to an area that is being redeveloped.

'Dance here for the spirits of this place which is to be knocked down. Dance them to a future place of light and harmony and peace. Dance their sorrow and dance their joy,' I was told.

Then I was taken to the top of Western Peak.

'Dance here for Hong Kong in the new century. Dance its past, its present and its future. Dance its coming difficult times and dance it through to calm and serenity.'

We managed to visit the Western Peak first. Christine wrote afterwards:

'The dance I did was lovely, soothing, gently flowing, singing the Blessing Song. I moved rather like Chinese dancing. Jane rattled around me the entire time, to keep me safe.'

Then to Stanley. As soon as Christine got off the bus she was aware of the spirits. She said:

'I found I was singing a very strong spirit song. This was the place I was to rattle and sing and dance. There was a sports ground behind us and we went in there. I was still singing. I invited Jane to join in and found that she was already singing the same song. It had come to both of us at the same time. We sang for ages. The song was full of grief and loneliness and fear. I wept and wept. Finally the song stopped.'

Exhausted, we went for a coffee. Then wandered around the famous Stanley Market while we slowly recovered our equilibrium. After a second coffee we went back to the area that was being demolished and sang again. Gradually this second song changed to a song of acceptance and a little hope for the future, although it was still sad. We promised that we would come back, and left. Two weeks later we went back. This time only Christine sang, a song of future peace. When the song was over we knew the work was done. This next piece is very hard to write. It is September 2001. A couple of days ago, on the 18th, I was writing the above passage. Suddenly I felt as if someone had just punched me in the stomach. I was feeling sick and dizzy and my ears were ringing. I looked at what I had just written and found that the last three times that I had intended to write 'Hong Kong' I had, in fact, written 'New York'. It was about half past three, BST. Almost exactly a week since the World Trade Center had collapsed. I Journeyed to find out what was wanted of me and was told,

'The spirits of New York need your help.'

I don't want anyone to think from this that I put steel and concrete before human souls. I don't. But I know, both from what my own spirits have told me and from Christine, that over the preceding week many, many people who can do this sort of work, as shamanic practitioners, spiritualists or in any other way, had been helping the souls of the dead in New York. When Christine had Journeyed to see what she could do to help she said:

'I was standing, with my Teacher, on top of the Chase Manhattan Bank. On every building that was still standing, for miles around, was someone doing the same thing as I was.'

But I am not a primarily a psychopomp. And the spirits had asked for my help. I asked my Teacher how they knew to ask me and he pointed out that doing work for buildings anywhere would be heard of, at some level, by buildings everywhere. All is connected.

So I went.

My Teacher took me to the roof of a building. I could hear screaming. My Teacher looked at me, seriously.

'Are the deaths that happened here worse than those of Indians dying in an earthquake? Or at Bhopal? Or of Serbs, Kosovans, Israelis, Palestinians?'

I thought about this, because I could see that he didn't want a trite answer. Then I said, slowly, 'No. I don't think they are. But I don't think they're better either.'

He smiled, sadly, and said, 'Then call the spirits that you have come to help.'

I called and they came, screaming, burning, trying to pull at me. My Teacher stepped in front of me.

'What do you think of all this?' he asked me.

'It makes me want to weep,' I said.

'Then weep.'

I did so. My tears fell in floods on the spirits and quenched the burning. Gradually they fell silent.

Then one asked, 'Are you crying for us?'

I nodded, unable to speak. They bathed in my tears until they were calm and peaceful.

Then they asked, 'What should we do now?'

My Teacher said, 'Go where you need to be.'

They streamed up, past me and into the sky.

My Teacher took my hand and we flew, first to the Pentagon where we did the same, then to the site of the crash in Pennsylvania.

'Now Kabul!' my Teacher said.

He took me over the Atlantic and over Europe. There were mountains. Then, as we flew lower, ruined buildings, beige against beige.

'Twenty-two years of war,' my Teacher said, in a matter-of-fact way.

I called out to the spirits and they came, old, weary and in pain. Unbidden, I began to cry again. At first they were angry. Then, as the tears touched them, they asked:

'Why is she helping us?'

My Teacher said, 'Because she cares. About every spirit and every soul. These are tears of love, pity and compassion. Accept them as they are given.'

They held out their hands and bathed in the tears. Then they flew up and past me into the sky.

CHAPTER NINE

RABBITS, JACKDAWS AND BLUE HARES

A short time ago I asked my students to ask their spirits to ...'show me the ways in which I have changed since bringing shamanism into my life.' There were, of course, as many ways as there were students. But all the changes had been for the better. This is Louise's Journey:

> *I went to the Upper World and my Teacher pulled an old, battered harp from behind a tree. He plucked at the few remaining strings to make an unpleasant, jangling noise. Then he played his new, shiny one. The music was beautiful.*
>
> *He said, 'I can show you hundreds of ways, like this one,' and he showed me a rough, choppy sea, followed by calm water with a yacht sailing regally across it.*
>
> *'Or this one.'*
>
> *There was a blizzard, blowing across a bleak moorland, followed by sunshine filling a green valley.*
>
> *'Or this.'*
>
> *There was a pile of rough, broken sticks followed by a shiny, polished staff. He went on:*
>
> *'You know how much has changed and will keep changing. You've climbed the highest hill now. All the rest will be gentler ups and downs.' He was quiet for a few moments as we looked out across the landscape and then he said:*
>
> *'Of course, it's not all a one-way street, you see. We learn from you as well. Everyone has their Teachers and helpers and some set out to find*

them and some don't. Some listen to their Teachers and some don't. I
suppose we are fortunate in that you have listened well to us. There is
mutual benefit.'

Louise's path had not always been easy, as you can tell from the
choppy seas, and the moortop blizzard. She had come through
depression and suicidal feelings, a great sense of worthlessness and
hopelessness. But she had been prepared to look at the aspects of her
life that were causing these problems and, with the help of her spirits,
she had come out the other side into the calm sea, the green valley.

Working on our own self-development is not easy. It is challeng-
ing, uncomfortable and hard. Often it can be unbelievably painful.
But, if we are to leave this life further along our spiritual path than
we started it, it is necessary. There are, of course, many ways of
doing it. I'm not saying that shamanism is right for everyone. But it
does have some very definite advantages. Your spirits can give you
not only advice, guidance and support but also help and healing.
And they do it with love and a great deal of patience.

People can have amazing adventures on their Journeys, and see
wonderful things. Sometimes these adventures and sights can be
hard to interpret. I am lucky in that, often, my spirits will sit me
down with a cup of tea and we will discuss whatever I have gone
there to ask them. We have had many talks about this book. I have
heard it said that everything that happens in a Journey is to be taken
literally and I would agree that everything that happens on a
Journey is real. Conversely, I have heard it said that everything the
spirits tell you and show you is symbolic. Use your common sense
on this one. If you have trouble interpreting a Journey, always look
back to what your intention was. This is the question that your spirits are concentrating on answering. And think, 'What does this
mean to me?' Journeys are not symbolic in the sense that you could
look up a meaning on a list. Suppose you were to visit, during a
Journey, a volcano. It would be sensible to ask yourself, 'What does
a volcano mean to me?', or to ask your spirits, 'What should I
understand by this? Please tell me in a way that I can understand.'
But a list in a book is not going to help you, nor is a friend saying,
' Volcanoes are about anger' or whatever. Of course, a friend saying,

'Didn't volcanoes come up in that Journey you did last spring? What did your Teacher say about it then?' could be *very* useful.

A couple of Journey messages that I have heard being discussed recently were:

'Help things to grow in your garden,'

and

'Get more sunshine in your life.'

Both of these can be interpreted literally as

'Do more gardening,' or

'Sunbathe and get some fresh air,'

or symbolically as,

'Nurture yourself and others,'

and

'Be happier.'

I find that the literal interpretation enhances the symbolic. If you get out into your garden and get dirt under your fingernails, then maybe other creative aspects of your life will get the nurturing they need. If you sit in the sun maybe it will make you happier.

A common version of this situation is where someone is told by his or her spirits to:

'Clear the clutter from your life.'

Does it mean from your head or from the cupboard under the stairs? May I suggest that you do both? Clutter in our heads or under the stairs blocks energy. And in that clutter under the stairs might be Great-Aunt Mildred's ornaments, which sat on her dresser for decades, absorbing all her anger and bitterness. Now they are giving that anger and bitterness off again, right in the middle of your home.

Some years ago Christine and I were given some jewellery by a woman who was mentally and emotionally ill. We accepted it because we were very fond of her, she was near death and we were happy to have things to remember her by. But the jewellery felt greasy and, when we looked at it in Non-ordinary Reality, we could see that it had dark and sticky webs all over it. We cleaned it with earth and water, as directed by our spirits, and, after a few weeks, it was clean enough to wear. Occasionally we have been given things that are too 'dirty' for us to keep. This has generally been when the

intention behind the gift was to bind us with obligation or grati-
tude. Then we either give them to someone who is not the target of
the intention (and therefore won't be bound) or we destroy them.
Most gifts are given with love and respect and we are able to accept
them with love and respect, but there are always the odd one or
two, as I'm sure you know, that will need cleaning.

Another good reason for the spirits telling us to get rid of clutter is that, as was pointed out by the house spirit in the seaside town,
people with cluttered houses often have cluttered minds.

However, there are few hard-and-fast rules when dealing with the
spirits. A few months ago we were asked to do some work in a house
in the next valley. Things had been disappearing, sometimes being
lost for months then turning up in the middle of the kitchen table.
There were strange noises and a feeling of hostility. The woman who
owned the house was scared. When we got there we discovered the
tiny cottage was crammed with objects. I had to Journey sitting in a
chair because there was no room to lie on the floor. When we went
into the bedroom Christine sidled in, closed the door and stood
behind it, then opened it again so that I could get in. There was no
other way for us both to get into the room. There was just enough
floor space for us both to stand. Every surface in the house was
covered in piles of books and papers, in ornaments and bric-a-brac,
from a long life of living in much bigger houses.

The house was haunted. The man who had owned the house
had stepped out of his door one day, into the road, and had been
hit by a car and killed. He was not aware that he had died and was
angry that a stranger was living in his house. He was responsible for
the hostility and the noises. But he did not seem to be moving
things around. Christine and her spirits took him to the Land of the
Dead, then I went to talk to the house spirit, whom I fully expected
to demand that the clutter be removed. But I was wrong.

'I love it,' said the large blue hare who was the spirit of the
cottage. 'There's always something new to look at. I'm sorry if I
scared her. I won't move things far and I won't damage them, but
tell her that I'll sometimes turn things around or rearrange them.
I'm not doing it to upset her. I just want to have a closer look at the
things. They are so interesting.'

Sometimes things that we are shown in Journeys (but not the Journey itself) are clearly symbolic. The woman who finds herself, on her Journey, swimming aimlessly around in circles may or may not be experiencing an allegory of her life. When this swimming comes in a Journey to ask a Teacher, 'What do I need to change in my life to walk more easily on my path?' and when it follows other Journeys in which her spirit helpers have shown her various alternatives and expressed disdain at those who work very hard to achieve very little and admiration of those who get their food in one burst of energy then relax during the day, the message is more likely to be about how usefully she spends her life, and in what balance, than about the relative worth of herbivores and carnivores.

One person may be told to slow down. Another, used to flopping in front of the fire with a good book, may be told to do more physically. 'Be still' is a common message, but so are 'get out more' and 'go for walks'. 'Go to the gym' is less common but not unknown. If we ask the spirits to help us to be balanced human beings then we must expect such messages. The only way to avoid sometimes getting answers that we don't like is to never ask the questions.

One of the most common instructions, so common that it can be treated as a bit of a joke, is 'Just be'. Remember, a thing becomes a cliché because it occurs often. If it occurs often it is because this is an important message that has a lot of relevance. It is hard to 'just be', hard even to have a clear idea of what it means or involves. It can take lifetimes of hard work, of cutting ties and making connections, of releasing fears.

A lack of connection leads to a lack of perspective and a lack of compassion. Connection and compassion are impossible without each other and without perspective. And yet, only in the experience of disconnection can we understand the value of connection. Only by experiencing fear and hatred can we work towards love. Maybe this is the true purpose of disconnection, that it is the starting point from which we move towards connection, love and compassion, all those attitudes that we hope will one day enlighten us.

Disconnection and conflict so often go together in our world. But, if disconnection has a purpose, does conflict? What is the importance of conflict? Well, think of omelettes and eggs. Without conflict nothing grows. There can be no birth without destruction. The goddess Kali creates and destroys, not as separate aspects but as the same aspect. If we never disagree with anyone and if no one ever disagrees with us then there is no learning, there is no growth. We need to be challenged and stretched.

This is not to say that suffering in famine or war is a good thing. You know, from the chapter on death, that some souls are reincarnated without having been able to absorb and learn from the mistakes and traumas of their past life or lives. And some of those souls have severe soul loss. Without complete souls we are not only more likely to wage war and to support the type of systems that allow some to starve and others to have more than they need but we are also less able to learn the lessons that we need to learn.

When we first realise the strength and help that the spirits can give us there is a great temptation to want to help others, regardless of whether or not they ask for our help. But to do this is to deny them the chance to learn their lessons. Once they ask, however, we must do what we can on a personal or global scale. Shamanism is, however, a local practice first and foremost. Quite frankly, I think we are often wasting time and energy when we try to do Journeys such as those to bring peace and prosperity to war-torn parts of the world. There are too many strong intentions to fight ranged against your intention for peace. If there weren't people wanting to fight then there wouldn't be wars. This is not to say that you shouldn't keep trying to persuade others that war is bad. At some point, if enough people come around to your way of thinking, then critical mass will be reached and wars will end. I keep hearing the question, during the Cold War, during Vietnam, through all the conflicts of the late-twentieth century to Yugoslavia and into this first conflict of the twenty-first century:

'When will we learn the lessons of previous wars and be able to live in peace with each other?'

It's a cry from the heart. When young men (and it is usually young men) go off to war they lose soul. Part of the soul that cannot cope with the situation of killing others and the possibility of being killed in such a way goes. If it is not returned then the young man goes through the rest of his life, maybe other lives as well, without that part of him that can least cope with a war. What is left is incomplete, more able to kill and fight. Of course, we have lessons to learn. Maybe the lesson of this is, at least in part, to look at ourselves first. Because we can only work on ourselves. Concentrating on what we need to change in ourselves, rather than on what we think should be changed in others, moves us forward on our paths and avoids the two big pitfalls of concentrating on others' faults. These are the pitfalls of despair and of smugness. Despair, because the problem is so big and we can easily start to feel powerless. In this situation we tend to give away power to others and then our troubles are compounded. And smugness because it is a rare person who can look at another's behaviour and think it wrong without feeling at least a little superior. 'If only everyone thought like I do!'

Recently the Drumming Group did a Journey to ask:

'How can I save the world?'

Twenty people came back with variations on:

'You can't. Work on yourself.'

A question to our spirits along the lines of:

'What can I personally do to help in this world situation?' at least focuses our attention, and that of our spirits, onto actions that are within our own ability. What can I do? What is my responsibility in this situation? Not, as I said before, because you are to blame but because, in taking responsibility to change those things that you can change, you are being a strong and power-full soul. And the ripples move outward. You can be an inspiration to others and a catalyst for change in others without ever realising it. If you nurture your own power without taking anyone else's you will have an effect on those around you.

To decide whether or not something is bad, as I have done above, is to make a judgement. Something that we all do all the time. We have a tendency to use words carelessly, while thinking we are being accurate. This causes many problems. Some words have specific and narrow definitions. We know the difference between a chair and a table, for example. A particularly experimental artist might wish to push back the boundaries of chair-table-ness, we might put out coffee on the chair or sit on the table, but we generally know the difference. That's the advantage of a concrete noun.

Bring in the abstracts and we are in a whole new ball game. 'Compassion', 'judgement', 'responsibility' and many others, are all words that get bandied about without a great deal of agreement as to what they mean. Dictionaries aren't much help. They are written by people who use these words in much the same way as the rest of us and dictionary definitions differ from one dictionary to another.

'No, no,' we argue, 'you're wrong. Compassion (or judgement, or responsibility) isn't like that at all! It's ...' and then we go into our own favourite definition – the one we feel comfortable with – as if we had the only true line of communication with the Great Dictionary-Master in the Sky.

There's a lot written about how we should be 'non-judgemental', without a great deal of explanation of what this means. Humans, on the whole, are not great abstract thinkers, whatever we like to believe. This is something that I have frequently talked with my Teachers about. A little while ago, as part of a Drumming Group, I asked my spirits to give me a guiding story for the drumming community. This is what they told me:

Tom had been in trouble at school again, so Jim, who hardly ever got on the wrong side of the teachers, had waited the half-hour detention in the cloakrooms so that the two boys could walk home together across the park. They stopped to lean on a railing and watch the three, black birds sitting on the tree branch.

'Look at those rooks in that tree,' said Tom.

'Are they rooks? I think they're crows,' Jim said.

'Naw, rooks. Rooks are always in groups. You just get crows by themselves or in pairs.'

'Could be ravens.'

Tom shrugged. 'Guess so. They're all pests anyway. Kill lambs.'

On the branch the crow turned to the other two birds and inclined her beak towards the brown, furry creatures at the foot of the tree.

'Those rabbits?'

The rook shrugged. The jackdaw shook his head.

'Could be hares. All the same anyway. Live in holes in the ground. That's unnatural.'

Below the tree the rabbit continued eating grass. The hare bade it goodbye and then loped off across the green.

Mrs Jones, walking her dog across the park thought, 'There's Jim Fisher with a friend. Nice lads.' She waved and they waved back.

Mrs Lee, going shopping, thought, 'There's Tom Smith with one of his cronies,' and tried to remember if she'd locked her back door.

My Teachers frequently tell me stories in order to get over a point that they want to make. In this case, of course, the point is about jumping to conclusions based on little evidence or knowledge. All people are individuals, with individual drives and motivations.

Unfortunately, most of us are so wrapped up in our own lives that, unless we are told directly that those we encounter have pains and problems of their own, we often assume they do not.

Judgement is not a bad thing. It's one of the things that keeps us safe. We use judgement every day – when we are crossing a road, for example, we judge how fast we can get to the other side and what speed the car approaching is going. We grow in judgement as we experience and understand those experiences. This is why more hedgehogs than humans are killed on the road and why children have more accidents than do adults.

Judgement is what lets us have opinions on situations, whether that is, 'Will United win the game on Saturday?' or 'Should we be deploying troops in…?' Without it we cannot function.

'But that's not what I meant!' you may shriek. 'I was talking about people!' Does this really mean that you'd trust the chap who is well known in the area for fraud with your life savings? We use judgement about people all the time.

The area that needs work is in when and how we apply that judgement. To judge from someone's clothes that they work in an office might be incorrect but it is based on experience. Being wrong gives us more experience that enables us to make a better judgement next time. To judge from someone's clothes that they 'aren't my kind of person' is based on prejudice, which is a totally different thing.

Perhaps a lot of the difference comes down to awareness. Awareness of why we have made a judgement. Awareness of the implications of that judgement. Awareness that we can always have made a mistake. Above all, awareness of the possible consequences if we act upon that judgement. All these take understanding of our society, of how and why others act as they do and, above all, an understanding of how and why we ourselves act as we do. All these require judgement in themselves. We learn about these things in the same way that scientists learn, or babies learn, or dogs learn. The same way that everything learns – it's the only way to do it. We have a theory and we test it. If the test results indicate that we are right, we hang on to that particular theory. If they don't, we modify our theory until we come up with something else that we can test. Of course, it is possible, easy even, to want to hang on to a theory into which we have invested a lot of energy. To throw out a theory means that we invite change into our lives and change is not comfortable. Change brings new life but it brings loss and death as well.

But if your main goal in life is to be comfortable then why on earth are you attempting to follow a spiritual path? Why are you here? Why are you reading this? We all need a rest now and again but, in order to move forward, we must step outside our comfort zone.

If we decide to be 'non-judgemental' we stop the whole thinking, experiencing process. We turn away from conflict, we stay in the comfort zone (or we attempt to. It doesn't work. Turning from conflict doesn't mean that conflict turns from you). If we make judgements with awareness then we are open to experience and can learn. If we simply stop, try to be 'non-judgemental' (is this even possible?) then we close ourselves off from experience. We never learn why Jim and Tom behave in the ways that they do, or why Mrs Lee is suspicious and afraid. We do not grow. We lose truth. And truth is something that we can rely on our spirits to give us. Whether that truth is comfortable or not. All we have to do is have the courage to ask for that truth. The courage to ask the question that could bring forth the uncomfortable answer. The courage to put aside the fear of change.

Judgement and compassion go together. Without the experience of both we can grow in neither judgement nor compassion. And either one must not stand alone. Judgement without compassion easily turns callous. And compassion without judgement becomes sentimentality.

I know that many people try to avoid conflict. Again this is part and parcel of the comfort zone mentality. How can you avoid conflict? Conflict exists.

Avoiding conflict means that the emotion is stored. It will grow and fester. Then you've got two choices. You can either carry on ignoring any situation in which the conflict might surface and, therefore, restrict your life, enjoyment and education or you can carry resentment until it explodes into far greater conflict than there was before. Better to have tackled it, with judgement and compassion, right at the start.

Not that I pretend this is easy. It isn't in the slightest. I'm working on it, daily. But the end result of being a balanced, compassionate soul whose actions are governed by love rather than by fear, although still a long way off, is a goal that I feel is worth striving towards.

CHAPTER TEN

WHERE DO I GO FROM HERE?

Now you've almost finished the book. I hope that you have enjoyed it. The answer to the question above is not always clear, since we all want something different out of our experiences and we each walk our own path. I can't, therefore, tell you that your next step is obviously to do an introductory workshop in shamanism. If that's the right answer for you then you probably know it by now, and don't need to ask.

Of course, finding a teacher of shamanism is not always straight-forward. Can I ask you to think about the answer to a question first?

What are you actually looking for in a teacher?

Are you looking for an all-wise, all-knowing guru who will never put a foot wrong and never step off the pedestal on which you have placed him or her? Because, if you are, you are likely to be disappointed. There are very few such paragons about. You may be thinking now:

'Of course not! What a stupid idea!'

But be honest with yourself. Many teachers disappoint and upset, sometimes even anger, students, simply by failing to deliver something that they never promised. No teacher has all the answers.

Of course, if the teacher you are drawn to *does* claim to have all the answers and to be an 'enlightened being' (and I have come across one or two who do) then on your own head be it. You could strike lucky and he or she might be right.

Most of us don't claim to be perfect and it can be irritating when students expect us to be. Be careful with this one. It's easy, when you look to someone to teach you, to demand more than you can reasonably expect.

And do you actually want someone to teach you shamanism or are you looking for (for example) 'Native American Spirituality'? Or 'Celtic Spirituality'? Or a blend of one of these and shamanism? There are some very good teachers around who can teach you any of these but, again, be honest with yourself about what you want. This is one of those times for telephoning the teacher and asking him or her all the questions you need to, before you go on the workshop.

Assuming the teacher is teaching what you want to learn, there are a few other things you might want to bear in mind. For example, who taught them? It may not be relevant and you may not have heard of the teacher's teacher anyway, but it's a guideline. How long have they been studying shamanism themselves and how long have they been teaching? Again, we each get to the stage of being ready to teach at different times but are you really going to trust someone who is only a few months on from their own introductory course?

Ask what is covered on the workshop. There are no right or wrong answers but better to find out now that the teacher is not covering shamanic Journeying than after you've parted with your money.

Does that teacher, or the organisation that he or she is representing, hold intermediate or advanced courses? It is a point to bear in mind that most teachers will only accept you on intermediate and advanced courses if you have done the introductory course with the same teacher or organisation. This is standard so don't be surprised by it.

Bear the same kinds of things in mind, particularly the length of time the person has practised, if you are looking for a shamanic healer.

Make sure that if you want shamanic healing that is what the practitioner offers. Practitioners will sometimes use shamanic ideas and language, such as soul loss, but will treat the problem in some other way, through hypnosis, guided visualisation or psychotherapy. Again, these methods are not wrong but they are not shamanism. Nor, for the main part, do practitioners of these methods pretend that they are. However, if you think that you need a soul retrieval and someone is offering 'soul retrieval therapy' it is easy to become confused. Be aware though that, although you may have decided that you need a soul retrieval, a reputable shamanic practitioner will go by what his or her spirits tell them to do, not by what particular aspect of shamanic healing you want.

Of course, at this stage, you may simply want to find out what other writers have to say about shamanism. In which case you will want to read more books. In libraries and bookshops shamanism can usually be found in one or both of two sections. Try both anthropology and 'New Age' or 'Mind, Body and Spirit'.

Those in the anthropology section will be, for the most parts, studies of shamanic societies in other parts of the world. I'm not going to mention many books by name – books can become out of print so quickly and choice is so individual – but I do recommend a few if you can't find any on the shelves and need to order. These are in the section 'Further Reading'.

In the 'New Age' section you will find books like this one. Books that are trying, with greater or lesser success, to get across the wonders and beauties of shamanism. Some of these will be 'how to' books. I said, in the first chapter, that I think a workshop is the best way to learn to Journey. If you can't get to a workshop for any reason, or you want to have a go with a book anyway, look at them carefully before you decide which one to buy. Read through the account of how to do the first Journey. Is it clear? Would you feel safe following the instructions? What does it suggest you do next? If there's only that first Journey in the book, are you are going to feel that you've been left high and dry? Students find it hard enough to know where to take their shamanism next when they have a teacher there to ask. It's even harder if you are learning from a book. And does the book take you onwards in safe, small steps? Make sure that it doesn't go straight from that initial Journey to sucking extractions or psychopomping. I know of two books that do exactly that!

Apart from these questions to bear in mind, the choice is really up to you. You'll learn something from almost any book – even if it is only to be more careful next time you spend your money – and you'll find things you dislike, disagree with or, at least, question, in even the best books. I check on three things when I am buying new books. The first is, 'Is this book really about shamanism, or is it about Medicine Wheel or Spiritualism or something else entirely?'

The second is, 'Does the author mention the spirits?' This may seem a strange question but I am often amazed at how much some authors write about shamanism without using the word 'spirit' once. There is a book on sale at the moment that refers to what I assume are spirits as 'entities of our consciousness'. Often they are presented as 'Higher Selves' or as aspects of our subconscious. If you are happy with this, okay. But without the spirits, shamanism cannot exist.

And the third thing I check is, does this book have a list of power animals and their meanings? If you find this in a book on, for example, Lakota spirituality and the meanings are the Lakota ones, then fine. But if it's a book purporting to be about shamanism generally, such a list has no place in it. What a wolf or a rabbit or a fox might mean to me, what those animal spirits might want to work with me on or help me with, will be quite different from what Wolf or Rabbit or Fox might mean to you. Any list, at best, is going to be either culturally based or the personal experience of the author of the book. At worst it will be made up along the 'everyone knows owls are wise' lines. Lists like these make me wary of the entire book. What else is made up? Is the list just to fill the last few pages? In my opinion, better to have a shorter, but better, book.

All right. You have been to your first workshop and you are raring to go! You'll want to practise. If you are lucky enough to have a friend or partner who is also working shamanically and you have a drum, then away you go! Most people just starting out on this path don't have either. This is where a drumming tape comes into its own. If you want to buy a drumming tape, then I should first ask the person who taught your workshop if he or she has any for sale. After all, you know that you can Journey to that person's drumming. Drumming speeds vary. They can be anything from about sixty beats per minute to about 240. Although as your experience increases you will probably learn to be able to Journey to almost any speed of drumming, to begin with you may well find some are too fast or too slow for you. If there are no drumming tapes available at the workshop, both the Foundation for Shamanic Studies and the North Yorkshire Shamanic Centre (addresses in the section 'Useful Addresses') sell tapes, as do many other shamanic organisations.

Look for ones that have a fifteen- to twenty-minute Journey for you
to use now and maybe a longer one for when you are more experienced. Make sure that it has a call-back, and check before you try it
for the first time that you know what the call-back sounds like.

Something else that I really recommend is joining a Drumming
Group. This is a group of people who meet to practise shamanic
Journeying. There are several around the country but, because there
is no central list, they can be quite hard to track down.

First of all, ask the teachers of the introductory workshop that
you attended. Even if they don't know of a group in your area they
may well be able to put you onto someone who does. *Sacred Hoop*
magazine (address in 'Further Reading') has a list of groups. Check
with the contact number before you turn up, since some groups are
closed or for students of a particular teacher. Check also that it is a
shamanic group. *Sacred Hoop* also carries listings for other types of
spiritual groups.

There are three newsletters/magazines that are worth a
mention. By far the best, as far as core shamanism is concerned, in
the UK, is *Spirit Talk*, a core shamanic newsletter that comes out
about three times a year. This is available from the same address as
Spirit Talk Workshops.

Sacred Hoop is a beautifully produced magazine appearing four
times a year. It describes itself as 'Shamanism and Ancient Wisdom
for Today's World', and covers many other native traditions and
practices as well as shamanism. It's well worth reading.

If you have a shop nearby that sells magazines from the USA you
might be able to get hold of *Shaman's Drum*, a journal of experi-
ential shamanism and spiritual healing. Relying on newsagents to
get American magazines can be rather frustrating. If you want to
subscribe, the address is in 'Further Reading'.

Whatever your next step is, I wish you as much wonder, as much
love and as many challenges as I have found in shamanism. May you
walk your path in beauty and joy, with your spirits by your side.

EPILOGUE

When I started this book, it seemed a huge task. Now, that task is almost complete. I've thoroughly enjoyed writing it, in spite of the hard work, and I've learned a lot from doing so. When I first started, it was obvious that I was going to need a great deal of help from the spirits and I went to talk to my Teacher. He took me to visit the spirit of this book.

> *The spirit was red and green, a small hunched figure who looked miserable. This was alarming, so I stepped closer. It looked up. No, it wasn't miserable at all. It was just thoughtful. It also looked a lot like me.*
>
> *'That's not surprising, is it?' asked my Teacher. 'You have to put a great deal of yourself into a book. Look at this spirit carefully. We need to bring the book and its spirit into manifestation.'*

I came back and, under instruction from my Teacher, made a model of the spirit in red and green polymer clay. Then I rattled over it, asking the spirit of the book to come into the model. When this was done I Journeyed again, to visit the spirit of this book.

> *'What do you want me to do, that will help you to come into manifestation?' I asked.*
>
> *'Make me a shrine beside your computer,' it answered. 'When you sit down to write, light a candle and a stick of incense. Come and visit me, along with your other spirits, when you get into difficulties. But, above all, you have to sit down and write. I know there are lots of more interesting things to do. When you are faced with a blank screen, even the washing up is more interesting. I can help but I can't write myself!'*

I did as I was told, although I can't pretend that I never procrastinated when it was time to write. I made the shrine, lit the candle and incense and printed out a poster for myself to go over my desk, which reads:

IT WON'T WRITE ITSELF!

Several times through the time the book took to write, its spirit encouraged and sympathised:

'I understand that it's much nicer to think about being finished than to work on finishing. But you could be a chapter further on by the end of the week!'

This week I Journeyed again to visit it and to ask if it and my spirits had any teaching or message for those people who would be reading the book. Here is what I was told:

'Live in the moment. Life is about now, not tomorrow. Exult that you have life, a very precious gift, and use it to enjoy everything you do – everything, even the bad, sad times. Enter into life as fully as you can and live.'

Appendix

Core Shamanic Practitioners' Circle Code Of Ethics

Permission – don't presume. Ask 'may/should I?' of both the client and the spirits.

Responsibility – own what is yours, hand back what is someone else's.

Payment – do not allow imbalance. Equally, do not deny help to those who need it and cannot pay.

Safe Space – provide a non-condemning space where the client can say what they need to. (This does not mean that we agree indiscriminately with the client, nor is it our job to collude in self-delusion.) If, for any reason, we cannot work, or continue to work, with a client we will do our best to find him/her another practitioner. The client has a right to expect honesty and compassion from us.

Confidentiality – where there is need to discuss a client (e.g. in order to ask advice of the Circle) do so with discretion and compassion. Where there isn't a need, don't.

Lack of Complacency – look regularly at your beliefs. Be prepared to let go of attachments.

Influence – be aware that, as a teacher or healer, you are in a position of influence. Do not abuse this.

Integrity – be honest about what you name yourself. Give credit to your teachers. Do not misrepresent your skills, knowledge, power or experience.

Useful Addresses

The following are some addresses of shamanic teaching organisations that hold workshops within the British Isles. (The Foundation is based in the United States. This address is their UK contact.)

The Foundation for Shamanic Studies
c/o The Sacred Trust, PO Box 603, Bath, BA1 2ZU

The North Yorkshire Shamanic Centre
29 Hill Cottages, Rosedale East, North Yorkshire, YO18 8RG
Website: www.nyshamaniccentre.co.uk
(The North Yorkshire Shamanic Centre is run by Christine Mark and me.)

The Scandinavian Center for Shamanic Studies
Artillerivej 63/140, DK-2300, Købanhavn S
Website: www.shamanism.dk
As you can see, this organisation is also based abroad. For details of their UK workshops contact *Kathy Fried (0208) 4593028.*

Spirit Talk Workshops
Karen Kelly, 120 Argyle Street, Cambridge, CB1 3LS
Karen does not teach introductory workshops. She is, however, happy to accept students on her courses if they have done an introductory workshop with one of the three organisations above.

The Foundation for Shamanic Studies runs courses across North America. Contact them at:
   The Foundation for Shamanic Studies
   PO Box 1939, Mill Valley, California 94942
   Website: www.shamanicstudies.org

Can I just mention the thorny problem of certification, here? None of the organisations above give certificates, either of competence or of attendance. I get asked about certificates fairly often and I know that there are teachers who give them. However glossy these look, they have no value outside the organisation concerned. If you want one and your teacher gives one, fine. But certificates say nothing about either your abilities or those of the person teaching you.

The procedure is much the same if you are looking for a healer rather than a teacher. There is no governing body in shamanism and no qualifications. Anyone can set up as a shamanic practitioner. You could, right now, even if the contents of this book are your only knowledge of the subject (please don't!). We've heard horror stories of people setting up as shamanic healers after an introductory workshop. It's difficult to know how many, if any, of these stories are true. But it does no harm to ask your potential practitioner who they trained with and what their experience is.

As I said, there's no governing body in shamanism. There is, though, a support group and professional organisation of practitioners working with core shamanism. At the moment it is very small but is intending to grow. This was set up by six friends who are all core shamanic practitioners and who include Christine, Karen Kelly (of *Spirit Talk*) and myself. We hold a list (again, small but growing) of practitioners known to us who are well trained and who are prepared to abide by a code of ethics, which is reproduced at the end of this book. You can contact us on (01751) 417795.

In addition, all the above teaching organisations will do their best to help you with any enquiries. Like most other shamanic teaching organisations, they will keep a list of students that they have trained in healing.

FURTHER READING

Among the books and magazines that I would recommend are:

BOOKS:
The Shaman, by Piers Vitebsky, published by Macmillan, 1995
   This is a small, glossy volume, packed full of information and photographs of shamans from all over the world. It's a very good book for helping you to decide what and who you might be interested in reading about next.
Shamanic Voices – a survey of visionary narratives, by Joan Halifax, published by Penguin, 1991
   A selection of testimonies, by shamans from all over the world, of their lives and work.
Shamanism – Archaic Techniques of Ecstasy, by Mircea Eliade, published by Arkana, 1989
   A classic work of anthropology.
The Way of The Shaman, by Michael Harner, published by Harper, 1982
   This is where Core Shamanism started.
Soul Retrieval, by Sandra Ingerman, published by Harper Collins, 1991
   About soul retrieval both in traditional societies and in Sandra's own work.

MAGAZINES:
Spirit Talk – The Editor, 120 Argyle Street, Cambridge, CB1 3LS
Sacred Hoop Magazine – Heddfan, Drefach Felindre, Newcastle Emlyn, Carmarthenshire, Wales, SA44 5UH
Shaman's Drum – PO Box 207, Williams, OR 97644, USA.

INDEX

Air 93, 94–6, 109
Animal spirits 19, 23–4
    see also Power animals
Animism 3
Archetypal places 65–7
Attachments 46, 88
Awareness, making judgements and
    155–6

Call-back 10
Cave of the Lost Children 65, 76
Change 9–10, 28, 33–4, 156
    and soul retrieval 49, 56, 57, 58,
    69–70
City, the 66–7
Cleaning gifts 149–50
Clutter 114, 149–5
Community
    shamans and 4–6, 27, 28, 30
    health and 38–9
    distant healing and 62
Compassion 151, 154, 156–7
Conditions, soul retrieval and 59,
    63–4
Conflict 151–3, 157
Connection 35, 151
Core shamanism 5, 162
Culture, shamanism and 4–6, 13–14,
    18–19, 27

Dancing 26
Demons 14, 16, 114
Disconnection 151
Dismemberment 28
Dominance, soul loss and 50
Dragon spirits 140, 141
Drumming 26
    tapes 161–2
    groups 162

Earth 93, 96–7, 109
Edge Land 88
Element meditation 25, 108–9
Elemental spirits 93–109
Elements, balancing the 98–101

Energy, unblocking 101, 103–5,
    137–40, 149
Extractions 33, 40–2, 46

Fasting 26
Fear 45–6
Fire 93–4, 109
Food
    honouring 17
    relationships with 26

Gifts 149–50

Hauntings 88, 110–128
Healing
    energy 33
    and the land 135–46
Hong Kong, healing work in 140–5
Hospital, the 76, 77–8
Houses
    house spirits and 110–128
    uninhabited 122–3
    cleansing 127
    honouring 127–8

Illness 27 28
    and change 34
    intrusions and 37–41
    spiritual aspects of 38–9
    power and 39–40
    as comfort zone 56
    contributing to 58–9
Integration, soul 64
Intention 70, 127, 130
    wording of 15–16
Intrusions 25, 33, 37–8, 40–2, 45–6

Journeying 3, 4, 11–12, 148–9
    intention and 15
    to Land of the Dead 76–7
    interpreting 148–9, 151
Judgements, making 154–7

Kabul, healing in 146

Land, healing and the 98–108, 129–46
Land of the Dead 29, 46, 67–8, 71–92
Land spirits 114, 129–46
Lost souls 37, 64–6, 67–8, 87–8
Love, healing and 34–5
Lower World 12, 13–16

Memories, soul retrieval and 62
Middle World 12, 16–18

New York, healing in 145–6
Non-ordinary Reality 6, 25, 26, 28,
  41, 88

Ordinary Reality 6, 14, 28, 41, 88
Orphanage, the 65–6

Personal growth 28, 29
Plants, spirits of 16, 17, 25
Poltergeists 105
Power animals 2, 10, 12, 15, 19–22,
  23–5, 34, 161
  intrusions and 46
  retrievals and 89–91
  Power
  giving away personal 35–6, 50, 70,
  15
  retrieval 36–7
Psychopomping 29, 88–9
Psychotropic drugs 25

Rainbow Bridge 86
Rattles 26
Reality, Ordinary and Non-ordinary 6
Reincarnation 80–3
Responsibility 154
River spirits 137
Robes 37

Sacred places, our perception of 135–6
Self-development 48
Shaman, criteria for being a 29–30
Shaman, initiation of 27–8
Shamanic healing 17, 23, 29, 31–46
Shamanic tools 19
Shamanic universe 12–30
Shamanism 2–12, 148
  choosing a teacher 158–60
  books on 160–1
  magazines on 162
Singing 26
Sonic driving 26

Soul
  number of 42
  stealing 50
  destination of 88–9
Soul loss 33, 35, 49–50, 70
  and intrusions 43–4
  anger and 60
  and the Land of the Dead 83
Soul parts
  keeping safe 55
  trauma and 64–6
  and the Land of the Dead 67–8
  and the Void 68
Soul retrieval 23, 33, 47–70, 129
  and shamanic practitioners 62–4
  after-effects of 64
  and the Void 69
Spirit
  realms 4
  helpers 23
  names 28
  soul and 105
Spirits 3, 18–19, 23, 161
  and intention 15
  Middle Earth 18
  shamans and 30
  of buildings 123–7
  nature of 131
  lost 133, 134–5
Spiritualism 4
Stones 96–7
Suicides 87

Teachers
  spirit 21–3, 78
  and Guides 23
  of shamanism 158–60
Trance
  mediumship 4
  states 13, 15, 17
Trauma 42–3, 49–50, 64
Truth 156

Upper World 12, 14, 16

Void, the 68–9, 84

War 152–3
Water 93, 97–8, 109
Workshops, shamanism and 10–12, 23,
  29, 138, 160
World Tree, Journeying and 13–14, 16